the side hustle gal

the side hustle gal

By Dannie Lynn Fountain

Published in the United States by Side Hustle Press

ISBN: 978-0692733127
ISBN: 0692733124

1. Entrepreneurship 2. Self Help, Creativity

Printed in the United States of America

Edited by Stuart Chapman

Book Cover Design by Copper Kettle Co.
www.ckc.io

For inquiries on speaking engagements, bulk orders
and more, please visit: www.sidehustlegal.com

book contributors

Melissa & Adam Schmidt of eMBee Events
www.embee-events.com

Cinnamon Wolfe of Cinnamon Wolfe Photography
www.cinnamonwolfephotography.com

Abagail Pumphrey & Emylee Williams of Think
Creative Collective www.thinkcreativecollective.com

Britny West of The Traveling Mindset Coach
www.britnywest.com

Kat Karpoff of Soapbox Creative Consulting
www.soapboxcreativeconsulting.com

Reid & Brittany Photography
www.reidandbrittany.com

Emily Walker of Chloe + Isabel
www.chloeandisabel.com/boutique/emilywalker

Kyrsten & Kelly Sherwood of Copper Kettle Co
www.ckc.io

Maggie Giele of Maggie Giele Digital Strategy
www.maggiegiele.com

Ashley Cox of SproutHR
www.sprouthr.co

contents

REACH: A step in the right direction.

GROW: Onward and upward we go!

a moment
of honesty...

I don't claim to have all the answers. Heck, one might argue I don't even have some of them. This is not meant to be a comprehensive guide to entrepreneurship, nor is it a book that'll build a business.

Businesses are built through hard work. Entrepreneurship takes determination. There will be tears. There will be doubt. There will be moments that you want to throw in the towel. Sleepless nights will become all too familiar. All of this is okay.

What this book is meant to be is community. Camaraderie. A place for you to feel less alone and know that you are not the first to face your struggles or fight your fights. Let's be that place together.

why "side hustle gal?"

The phrase "part time entrepreneur" is a misnomer. As written, it means someone who pursues entrepreneurship on a part time basis. However, this phrase is commonly used to refer to those entrepreneurs that have other commitments that prevent them from focusing solely on their entrepreneurial pursuit as a career. They might still have a 9-5 job, they might be a parent, or they might simply have responsibilities that inhibit the amount of time they have.

However, these individuals are by no means committing "part time" effort to their business. In fact, typically they contribute just as much time to their business as they do whatever it is that keep them from pursuing entrepreneurship full time.

Enter the Side Hustle Gal. This phrase more appropriately defines the large group of women who are pursuing entrepreneurship. They may have one of those commitments mentioned above or perhaps they have no interest in being a full time entrepreneur, and that's okay too. **This book is for you.**

open: you just have to get started.

what does it mean to be a side hustle gal?

Memoir by EMBee Events

After almost 15 years as a Managing Editor of peer-reviewed medical journals, I can honestly say that I feel competent and confident in my job. Feeling confident is a wonderful thing: I have a depth of experience that gives me a certain amount of personal joy, and I feel proud when I consider my career path. The job lends itself well to my Type A tendencies (for those of you who watched Friends, I'm "a Monica," as I imagine many of you reading this book are), and I daresay that I feel good at it. Every woman should have something in her life that makes her feel accomplished, skillful, and proficient.

Don't I sound comfortable? Now, if you have an extra few seconds, read that paragraph again. Did you hear me say I love my job? That I'm passionate about it? That I can't wait to wake up and go to work every day? That it lights a fire in my soul and makes my eyes sparkle? Every woman should have those things, too.

Here's the challenge: What happens when your job – the one where you're skillful and experienced, confident and qualified – is too comfortable (either financially or emotionally) to walk away from, but it also doesn't bring you the passion or joy that you imagine a creative business would?

I graduated college in 2002 after 3 years of hard work, with a degree in English. I had big dreams: I was going to move to New York and become an Editor at Random House, a la Jacqueline Kennedy Onassis in her later years, surrounded by a sea of genius books for which I could be the midwife, birthing them into the consciousness of voracious American readers. (Man, that would have been a fancy job.) Or maybe I was going to get my PhD and teach English literature at Brown, or Berkeley, or some other beautiful school where people's intellectual passions were more important than bread and water. (Or Ramen, on a student's stipend.)

Looking back with an honest eye, I'm not sure I knew what I wanted to do, but I knew the feeling I wanted to have: adulthood. I wanted a career, not a job. I wanted to make it on my own. I wanted independence, passion, financial security, and influence. I wanted to make a mark. On my way to the Big Dreams, I figured I'd better get a "small dream" kind of job, so I started searching even before I finished my B.A.
As luck would have it, a major peer-reviewed journal in my town had a new Editor-in-Chief, and he was looking for a Managing Editor to help him set up his office. He thought "Managing Editor" meant "secretary"; all I could think was that it was title on the masthead at Random House. We were a match made in...well, not heaven.

In truth, I'm forever grateful for that big break, such as it was. At 21 years old, I had a title many people work half a career for. It was an incredible opportunity, and one that has since taken me all over the world, where I've met all sorts of both wonderful and intelligent people, and it has kept me gainfully employed and well-fed for 15 years. It has even brought me moments of great excitement and passion, as the publishing industry has faced many crises – and therefore creative opportunities – in the last decade.

Still, it doesn't make me feel wild in the way life should. For many of us, our parents come from a generation where work was just that…work, and not necessarily a career. It was a means to an end. But somewhere along the way, the work ideal – at least for many of us –became something different. The Dream, no matter what floats your boat – is for your passions and your work to match as closely as possible. Doing what I love for work (and money if possible) is the ultimate goal for me…and I'm sure it is for you, too, or you wouldn't have picked up this book.

However, again: What happens when your day job is too lucrative to leave? Sometimes, "lucrative" means money, but sometimes it means stability in other forms. I'm reminded of a cartoon, Dilbert I think, where each time an employee wants to quit, his manager puts a brainwashing contraption on his head and he keeps repeating "Health insurance," "parking space," "free coffee" until he decides to stay. As funny as that might be, it's often true.

The long and short: Sometimes your day job is just too crucial to the business of life to leave it. (At least for now.) This situation presents a special set of challenges, of course. As a Side Hustle Gal, you already know that. Continuing to work during the day and pursuing your passions in your off time can be exhausting, no matter how excited you are about your side project. If your employer knows about your side gig, you might even get the side eye; how do they know you're not doing other work while you're on the job? And perhaps most difficult, how do you maintain commitment to (and a measure of enthusiasm) for your Real Job when your heart is with the side gig?

My husband (who also has a Real Job as an attorney) and I are on the early part of this journey. We've opened a wedding and event planning company, which has been a dream of mine for about a decade. I told myself I couldn't do it because (a) it was too different from my education and my existing career path, and (b) I'd never have the time or energy to do it while holding down a full-time job, and (c) my full-time job was too good to quit in exchange for something so financially unpredictable and scary. I'm not going to argue with any of those points, because they're all true. I just got tired of letting them stop me.

I did wait, though, until the timing was right. We have two incomes. We don't yet have kids. Between me and my husband, we have a huge network of people who can support us and connect us with the vendors, clients, and collaborators we need to make this work. I truly believe that if I'd tried to do this 10 years ago, my Side Gig would have eaten my Real Job (and me) alive. Now, I am confident and competent (most days, anyway) in my ability to balance and prioritize my work well enough so that nothing has to go on the chopping block until I decide it does.

If you're in the same situation as me, where your career is too lucrative to leave, this is what I have to say: Don't. There are so many merits, financial and otherwise, to keeping a day job.

Here's how I think of it:

Your "main" career can give you confidence, resources, skills, and experience that will translate to your side gig.

Your "main" career keeps money coming in the door, which means you get to pursue your side gig on passion alone at first. That's an exciting thing. Plus, it keeps the pressure off. You might lose momentum or enthusiasm if you needed your side gig to keep the lights on.

Your "main" career, if you do it right, can even benefit from the creative flow you feel when you're working on your side gig. Think how much time you probably spent daydreaming about doing it before! Now, you actually are. You can focus on work when you're at work, and your passion when you're off work.

It can be daunting, but I find great joy in this Side Gig sisterhood. The grass isn't greener over there, my friends. It's green on our side, too – because we can pay to water the grass.

- Melissa Schmidt

Melissa Schmidt is the Co-Founder and Owner (with her husband, Adam Schmidt) of eMBee events in Atlanta, Georgia. As event designers and coordinators, Melissa and Adam work with brides to make Southern wedding magic: they help bring to life the kind of events where guests leave feeling warm, happy, loved, and inspired at the end of the night. You can find them at www.embee-events.com.

The Side Hustle Gal movement all started with a book. I had a novel idea (pun intended) to put together a guide to all the resources I've collected and lessons I've learned over the years while running a business. Part time entrepreneurship is hard and I thought that if I could save some time for amazing women like you by collecting these resources all in one place, I'd have found a way to give back to the world.

As all projects do, the Side Hustle Gal has become so much bigger than that. I talk to women every day that struggle with entrepreneurship. I hear things like:

- "I don't have downtime because my downtime is spent editing photos"
- "I love my day job, but mostly because it gives me the capital to work on this entrepreneurial thing"
- "Man, I'm really burnt out but if I stop working, I'll never be at a place to get this entrepreneur thing to be my full time gig"
- "Somehow we've all bought into this notion that life isn't life and we can't enjoy it and live out our dream if we are handcuffed by a 9-5 job."

In fact, Cinnamon Wolfe wrote an entire blog post on the way part time entrepreneurs feel as though they are less than full time entrepreneurs. That hurt - but it hurt because she's right. There's this perception that to be a "real" entrepreneur, you have to do it full time. Not all full time entrepreneurs feel this way - in fact, some of the memoirs you'll read throughout the book are from full time entrepreneurs - it's simply a perception that we as women have talked ourselves into.

I'm here to tell you that every. single. female. entrepreneur. is worthy. We are all strong. We are all brave. Entrepreneurship (regardless the shape, form, size, or color) is hard. Entrepreneurship is not for the weak. I'm here to tell you that I own two successful businesses (LE Consulting and Side Hustle Gal), I'm a partner in a third, and I still have a full time job. Heck, just a few short months ago, I was juggling two businesses, a full time job, **and grad school**. I'm not alone in this either, so many women that are a part of the creative entrepreneur community are Side Hustle Gals. Some don't even know they are, like the woman that bakes cakes on the side and thinks of it as a paid hobby.

The truth is that women who are part time entrepreneurs (and I really do believe that word is a misnomer) are ROCKSTARS. We are strong. We are capable. It's time we stand together and recognize that we are a force to be reckoned with.

basic
business management

Memoir by Cinnamon Wolfe Photography

It's ok to have a 9-5 job, I promise. I'm departing slightly from my usual nerdy teaching conversation to talk about something that I've seen happening in our community. Granted, we all run in different circles and so you may not be as aware of this as I have been depending on your current "circle", but if you spend any amount of time hanging out where other small creative and online business owners hang out, you might have noticed it too.

Your "dream" isn't really a dream unless you ditch the 9-5.

And I'm here to tell you friends.... that's a big fat lie. Somehow we've all bought into this notion that life isn't life and we can't enjoy it and live out our dream if we are handcuffed by a 9-5 job. Where in the world did this come from? Wasn't the dream from a while back to actually HAVE a job that would allow you to support yourself and your family?

Now, I'm not saying it's a bad thing if your goal is to quit your 9-5 job and support yourself 100% though your own business. What I AM saying is that it's not the ONLY thing.

And I feel like (to an extent) our creative community has forgotten this.

Sure, there is beauty and something to be learned from those who give it a go and make it work (thanks Tim Gunn) in full time small business entrepreneurship. But there is also beauty and something to be learned

31

from those who juggle two different gigs, or a gig and being a full time-mom, etc.

Your story may look different from their story, but that doesn't mean your story is wrong.

Let me tell you a little bit of my own story....For anyone who doesn't know the backstory on how I became a photographer...it kind of happened as a result of pure circumstance. I don't have stories of me carrying around a camera everywhere I went as a 5 year old. I didn't dream of being my own boss or capturing love stories while I was slaving away at a corporate job.

I received a Master's Degree in Human Resources from the University of New Mexico in 2004. I worked my way up to what I would consider a fantastic job at T-Mobile as Human Resource Business Partner throughout the next 8 years. I taught a few classes at UNM and also at Bellevue College on Organizational Behavior and Performance Management. I loved what I did, I was good at it and I aspired to do more especially in the area of teaching.

Then the Army moved us to California. To a tiny little town with no "big" HR jobs. It wouldn't really work for me to work remotely. I wasn't horribly depressed about this but I was a little trepedatious. What in the world would I do now?

Backing up a few years....I got my first pink Canon point and shoot digital camera when I was planning a trip to Japan in 2007. I loved that camera and enjoyed taking photos that focused on interesting compositions rather than just pointing and shooting.

5 years later as I sat in a friends house in California, jobless, I looked at her new-ish DSLR camera sitting on her kitchen table and thought, "Hey I have all this time now, I should learn how all this photography stuff actually works!"

And that was the start. That was the birth of Cinnamon Wolfe Photography. I devoured every resource available. I read and read and read and read some more. I got a Canon t3i and practiced all the time. I practiced on some friends and started thinking....I have a business background...is it that impossible to think I could actually turn this into something?

And I did. ***Or, I am?***

I guess I will always be...turning it into something, since owning your own business never really slows down or stops. You need to continually grow. Continually learn. Continually deal with things that get thrown at you (moving your business across the country anyone?)

That literally makes my heart want to cry.

There is NOTHING wrong with having a job that pays your bills. There is nothing wrong with having a job and a creative business "on the side". There is nothing wrong with ENJOYING BOTH.

Why do I tell you this story? Because sometimes (actually maybe a lot of the time?) I wish I could just go back to that cushy 9-5 job.

Yes, I said that out loud.
I know of someone who actually HID the fact that she had a 9-5 job from industry friends (FRIENDS!!!) because she didn't want to appear like she didn't have enough of her stuff together to be full-time fancy.

I know that personally, I have struggled with feeling like if I ever have to go back and "get a job" that would mean I am an utter and total failure at life and everyone else around me would be "living their dreams" while I had to "go back to work."

That literally makes my heart want to cry.

There is NOTHING wrong with having a job that pays your bills. There is nothing wrong with having a job and a creative business "on the side". There is nothing wrong with ENJOYING BOTH.

We all have different goals and aspirations and dreams. Some of that may include being a full-time entrepreneur and some of that may include doing a full time job and another part time job at the same time. We need to be able to give each other (and ourselves) grace to be who we are and pursue what we think is best for our lives.

I didn't choose to become a full-time photographer...it happened by accident. We are in a place right now where I don't have to pursue a different full time job outside of what I do in my business but let me tell you there are certainly times when I would rather just go to work and do my work all day and then come home and read a book! Or watch TV without feeling like I should be "working on my business".

Because let me tell you friends, it doesn't stop. Its ALL you, ALL the time and there really are no breaks. It's hella hard to give yourself the ability to have some down time or off time because social media is screaming in your face that you.will.never.catch.up with what so-and so is doing.

But here's the thing. You don't HAVE to catch up. You don't HAVE to do what they did. You have your own wins and successes and even though you might think this is silly...there are people out there thinking they will.never.catch.up with YOU.

To every single person who has a "corporate job" or a 9-5 and they think that it's dead-end and horrible....or even those who feel like in order to be seen as a "success" or "legit" that they have to give that job up.....I'm here to tell you, your DREAM doesn't have to be the same as everyone else's.

Entrepreneurship is flat out hard and not everyone who starts down the path will end up in the same place. Evaluate what you really want to accomplish and WHY you want to accomplish it and then take action to get you there. If that means you keep on thriving in your day job, then by all means...rock it out and don't let anyone else make you feel bad because of it.

That's it friends. I hope that some of this was an encouragement and inspiration for you to really understand what it is that you want to do and the path you choose to get there will always be your path, not someone else's.

- Cinnamon Wolfe

I'm Cinnamon (for reaslies!) and I provide joyful wedding photography for the seriously awesome couple. I am an avid celebrator of marriage and am obsessed with blogging, my pups, hot coffee and cold diet coke and my heartthrob of a husband, Paul. When I am not behind the camera, you can find my fingers burning up the keyboard, my nose in a book or maybe just on the couch enjoying some Netflix! I am absolutely nothing without amazing grace. I am a fun introvert (its a thing, I promise!) who loves people and there is nothing I enjoy more than laughing with and serving couples that entrust me with their memories. You can find me online at www.cinnamonwolfephotography.com

When beginning to run a business, there are a multitude of tasks that need to fall into place nicely to ensure that things go as smoothly as possible. It may be nice to focus on the passion part of your business - the photography, the crafting, the design work - but it's important to not lose sight of the administrative tasks. In order to set you up for success, these are my recommendations for getting started and managing your business more effectively. This will make sure you're always on top of things.

SELECTING A BUSINESS TYPE

Once you've had an opportunity to begin developing your business, it's time to consider registering it to give yourself some additional protections. It's time to consider a Sole Proprietorship vs. a Limited Liability Company. What's the difference and which is best for you?

First, make a list of things that you need (do you need to protect your assets from potential lawsuits? Are you in a position to incur additional expenses while setting up your business?) and then consider which business formation type aligns best with your needs based on the description below (and seek legal advice from a proper business advisor, of course).

Sole Proprietorship. There is no legal distinction between owner and business with a sole proprietorship. It is inexpensive to form, and manage. However, you cannot sell or transfer the business (something to consider for the future) and it can only be made up of one person. Furthermore, the owner is 100% liable for any and all losses or lawsuits that might arise throughout the course of doing business. Sole proprietorships are the least expensive business type when it comes to tax time. Sole proprietors simply file a Schedule C along with their standard Form 1040. There are a few additional forms if depreciation or other business matters come into play, but other than that, it's pretty "standard".

Limited Liability Corporation (LLC). An LLC combines properties of a partnership and a corporation and the owner and business are two separate entities. This means that you're only liable for what you've invested in the business. The ",LLC" after your business name also tends to lend credibility to your business name. Taxation is up to you, you can choose to be taxed on your tax return (if a single-member LLC) or as an entity. If you are a single-member LLC (meaning there is only one "owner" of the LLC) you can still file taxes as you would if you were a sole proprietorship (you just get the added benefits listed above). Essentially, LLCs are treated the same as sole proprietorships for taxes – the company itself doesn't pay taxes, the individual members pay taxes on their share of the company's net profits. However, LLCs are more expensive to form, manage, and pay taxes on and can be made up of one or more people.
Which form is the best for your business?

FILES AND ORGANIZATION

As a business owner, staying organized is an absolute must. I recommend two main ways of staying organized (and I implement both in my businesses).

Hard-Copy Binder: For all important paperwork, like EIN letters, LLC filing papers, and even the copyright certificate for this book, I put the originals in clear sleeves in a single binder, with a tab for each of my businesses. This binder is my go-to resource whenever I need anything for my businesses and I love that everything is in one place.

"staying organized is an absolute must for new and seasoned business owners."

Digital Backup: If you have email for your business through Google Apps for Work, that also means you have 30GB of storage. Create a folder for your business in Google Drive and subdivide it into the following sections:

1. Taxes
2. Important Business Documents
3. Business Operating Procedures
4. Business Resources
5. Client Contracts

In the taxes folder, save a PDF of each of your annual tax returns (and quarterly payment documentation, if applicable). In the important business documents folder, save scanned versions of all the original documents in your hard copy binder. In the Business Operating Procedures folder, you should keep all the living documents of your business (I have these all as Google Docs or Google Sheets so that they're easy to update during my bi-annual processes reviews). In the business resources folder, save all of those PDFs, free e-books, etc that you download when you sign up for an email list – I go through and purge these about once every three months or so. In the client contracts folder, save the final signed PDF contract from each project you take on, even if you have a client management system like HoneyBook that you use.

PLANNING AND CALENDARS

Missing a meeting is my absolute worst nightmare. I hate to be the person to waste someone's time or otherwise mess up the flow of their day. For me, that means I've become an incredibly planful person, integrating Google Calendar and a paper planner together to create the best system for me.

There are thousands of planners out there on the market and dozens of digital planning tools as well. It doesn't particularly matter which one you choose for your business, so long as you choose a planning tool and stick with it. For convenience and streamlined processes' sake, I do recommend using Google Calendar if you're already using Google Apps for Work.

CONTENT

Plan your content in advance. Running your blog, website, and social media is a large part of your business (see Chapter 3 for more on this). It's how you show your ideal clients and readers that you know what you're talking about and that you love what you do. Blogging and sharing content on a regular basis is an essential part of this. If you create a blog schedule and stick to it, you not only create a consistent stream of content, your readers also know you are someone they can depend on to do the work they might hire you for every single week.

Plan your content using themes. Grouping similar topics together in monthly themes will keep your readers and potential clients coming back for more and begin to build a loyalty loop. It's also possible to break large topics such as "Social Media Management" into smaller chunks and address each separately. Following the same example, you can create topics around Facebook, Twitter, Pinterest as well as topics around the best tools for scheduling social media posts or managing your bank of content. Start with broad themes, brainstorm, and pick the more specific themes that align best with your audience after. It's the perfect way to dive deeper into the topics you cover.

Quick tips for content planning. Be sure to pick monthly themes and brainstorm content that suits those themes. Pick topics that complement each other or build your readers' knowledge one post at a time. Ensure that the topics you select align with your audience and answer questions they might have. Choose monthly themes that complement and build on one another. Make sure you create a content plan for two to three months at a time, that way you can see where you're working towards. Put your topics ideas away for a day or two, and come back to them with fresh eyes. When you're picking out topics you're going to use on your blog, that's when your inner critic gets to come in and give his opinion.

plan: all the best
things started
with an idea

marketing 101

Memoir by Think Creative Collective

If you had to ask us what makes a business successful, we wouldn't say the colors mattered, or the type of photography, or even who you were marketing to. In fact how you do business is irrelevant. What you sell is irrelevant. How you reach your ideal client is (slightly) irrelevant. What matters most, hands down, is your consistency. You should be consistently predictable. Your people should know where to find you, when to find you and have a general idea of what to expect when they get there. How you look, how you talk, even the frequency in which you communicate should be consistent. Consistency doesn't mean boring. It doesn't mean you can't be unexpected or even surprise your dreamies from time to time. But your consistency will build a trust that can't be denied.

We built and marketed our business based on this consistency factor. You could find us on our blog, Instagram and in our Private Facebook Community. Our pins run rampant on Pinterest. And we are known for the ridiculous amount of online training we offer for free.

Our consistency has given us a reputation. The kind of reputation we are willing to stand behind. We get tagged in pretty pictures of succulents and bouquets of blooms - because people know we love them. Find a goofy photo of an animal (yes, even porcupines) with a birthday hat on and we are a tag away. This consistency has given our audience a little glimpse of who we are. We show our authentic selves on and offline.

Creating this consistency isn't always easy. As creatives, there are a lot of things we love (new fonts, image styles, graphic icons), but we knew that if we stuck to what our brand was about it would pay off. Try creating a moodboard of everything that encompasses your business and brand. Put pictures of food, outfits, colors and textures that match the look and feel of your business. What do you want people to feel when they interact with your business? What's your color scheme and vibe? It'll be easier to always be able to go back to that foundation when the next "shiny object" tries to catch your eye.

We'd love for you to get inspired by the brand we've created!

- Emylee Williams & Abagail Pomeroy of Think Creative Collective

At Think Creative Collective it is so much more than just a cute Instagram feed or being popular. We strive to harvest a community built on giving. You can sit with us. We are about helping businesses become brands that make a difference. We strive to create a path to achieving your goals. And reward yourself with a purposeful and profitable business. We'll give you the kick in the butt you've been needing to grow your business, simplify and streamline your life. You can find more about us, upcoming workshops and our latest Instagram crush by heading to www.thinkcreativecollective.com.

When it comes to getting your message out there, there are a lot of people that claim they have 'the right way', but what is the best way for them isn't necessarily the best way for you. There are a lot of different routes and options to choose from when deciding the best way to connect with your ideal clients. Marketing, Social Media, PR and advertising all bring something to the table. So what is the difference between each and how do you know which one is the best for you?

The two that cause the most confusion are **Marketing and PR (Public Relations)**. While they might sound like the same thing to start off with, they serve different purposes. The biggest difference is that marketing is what you use to get your customer acquainted with the product and eventually buy it, whereas PR focuses on creating relationships with customers, media and other people that support your company and its values.

When looking at **marketing vs. advertising**, one might ask the same question. How are these two different? Marketing is everything you do to get your product or service noticed and a marketing plan consists of several different factors. Advertising is one part of the marketing plan, such as the ads you see on Facebook, in magazines, and on television.

Last but not least we have **social media**. This can be used for several different facets of marketing, PR and advertising. It's a super useful tool that you can use to get your service out there while building relationships with your customers at the same time.

MARKETING

Effectively marketing your business requires a marketing plan, a timeline for execution, and clear goals to mark progress.

Create a marketing plan. With any business and marketing plan, start with knowing who your ideal client is. Where do they congregate, what do they love, and most importantly, what do they need? Why do they need your product or service and how will it help them.

Determine your marketing style. What works for one business, doesn't mean will work for the other business.

SOCIAL MEDIA

Social media is a broad term that covers a large range of platforms. Not every platform is right for each business. If you have a more visual based business, platforms like Instagram and Pinterest might be better. If your business is more text-based, Facebook or Twitter would be more aligned with your goals.

Twitter. Twitter is short, sweet and fast. With messages that consist of 140 characters and millions of users, a Twitter timeline changes fast. If you don't keep a constant eye on your timeline, there will be hundreds of new messages to read every time you log on. It's both a strength and a weakness of Twitter. It's a strong tool because you can fire away a lot of messages about your product and service without getting annoying and salesy, but it's weakening because your message gets lost in the crowd quickly. Twitter is also a great platform to share messages from other entrepreneurs and those of your clients. Retweeting encourages community.

Facebook Groups and Pages. There are two ways to use Facebook for your business. You can set up a Facebook page to keep your clients and customers informed of what you do while also sharing content with the larger world. You can also set up a Facebook group to really interact with your audience and build a loyal community.

A Facebook page is the easiest way to share what's going on in your business. You can share the blog posts you write, share client responses, when you have a sale, share behind the scenes photos, or even share content that is useful to your audience. It's a quick and easy way to show what you are up to and give your potential clients an extra way to reach you.

In a Facebook group, it's all about interaction. Here, your audience and potential clients have the space to form a community. They can ask you questions, share how they use your products or chat about a common interest. You can still share behind the scenes from your business, but maintaining a group is much more work and it will take a lot more commitment – one that will be worth it if you value a lot of interaction with 'your crowd'.

Instagram. Instagram is like Twitter with images. You can follow and tag people, and your timeline consists of a stream of images created by those you follow. Crisp images do well here, Instagram is a place for beauty. The prettier the images, the more likes it has the potential to get and the more followers you will gain. It's also possible to write a long caption to go with the image and add hashtags to make the images more easily found by your ideal client.

Instagram is also a place to engage. It's a place to appreciate the community that beautiful images can create. It's a place where you can be honest and real about your business struggles in more than 140 characters.

Pinterest. Pinterest is also all about images, but while Instagram is dominated by square images, long portrait images work really well on Pinterest. Again, bright, crisp images seem to be the key here. The more visually appealing, the more repins, shares and even clicks to your website you will get. Unlike Instagram, you can link each Pin directly to the post or somewhere on your website. If you'd like for your audience to repin images from your website, be sure to maximize the "alt tag" section of your pictures - this text will be the default caption for your Pinterest post.

Periscope and Snapchat. Periscope and Snapchat are distant cousins and they represent the Wild Wild West of social media. These platforms are all about instant gratification, quick-hit messages, and fast content. They're a place where you can share a more "insider" message, because the content doesn't last forever. They're also an appropriate place to get more personal, for the same reason.

YouTube. Vlogging is booming business at the moment – even more than blogging it seems. Though the two seem to go hand in hand. Bloggers start a vlog and visa versa. It's the perfect way to create extra content for your blog, or show more personality and 'you'. It's also a great way to share behind the scenes or to add a video tutorial to your step-by-step post.

PRESENCE & STRATEGY

The difference between presence & strategy. When it comes to social media, it's common to hear about a social media presence and a social media strategy. While they mostly go hand in hand, there is a slight difference between the two. A social media presence is everything you do on social media. You show up, share posts, are helpful to people, retweet their content, and share your own.

A strategy is slightly different. This is a plan you set up to create a good social media presence. How often do you want to share your own content? How many times will you be tweeting about other people's content and how many hours will you spend on social media? While you want to build up a good social media presence, the strategy is what will get you there.

Finding a strategy that works for you

Make friends, be helpful & don't sell at every opportunity. One of the best ways to gain followers is to be known as an expert. Be helpful, share content created by your followers, share content that you think might be helpful for them. If there's anything that people hate more than people constantly talking about themselves, it's people you only hear from when they have something to sell, or during launches. Don't be that social media user. Be helpful, and genuinely interested in the other person, business or product. Sharing someone else's content won't take away from your traffic, instead it will give you brownie points with other entrepreneurs and will show your audience that you're not above community.

"make friends, be helpful, and don't sell at every opportunity."

ADVERTISING

Social Media Ads. Social media ads can be an incredible way to target specific people or groups and grow your reach or build your list. Facebook's ad manager provides in-depth ways to target, from looking at your competitors to common interests, and everything in between. There are so many courses out there on social media ads – dive into one today and try out a new skill!

Advertising on blogs. Are you a calligrapher? Give advertising on wedding blogs a try. You'd be amazed at the kind of reach you can get by specifically targeting places where your ideal client is a reader. The same can be said for a marketer advertising on a web design blog, an artist on an interior design blog, and other similar correlations.

Sponsored posts. Sponsored posts are the sweet spot of advertising. Often called "brand stories" today, these editorials are ways to tell your story in an authentic way that comes across as relationship-building rather than promotional. Many magazines (such as Belong Magazine) and blogs (such as Refinery29) offer sponsored post/piece opportunities.

PUBLIC RELATIONS

This is all about creating relations, getting your message out there and showing some personality. This is the part where you're nice, helpful and approachable for people. Show they you have their best interest at heart and that you really care about them as well. It's also really important that you place yourself as a figure of authority here -someone who knows their stuff and who knows what they are talking about. There are several ways to do this.

Guest Posts. Find out where your people hang out. Which blogs (the bigger the better!) do they read a lot. What kind of information are they looking for and what kind of questions do they have.

If you know the answers to these questions, it's time to start pitching those bigger (authority) blogs with an article that will help their audience (who also happens to be yours). The more specific here, the better. Let the blog editor know what type of article you want to write, the outline of the article, a proposed headline and why you are the best person for the job.

Hi [name],

I loved your blog on [topic], because [reason]. It really stood out to me. After following your blog for a while, I've noticed that you don't have posts on [name topic where there is a content gap]. How does this post sound: [awesome topic title]? In this post, I will [short and to the point outline of the post]. Your readers will love this because [reason].

I am [name] and I'm an expert on [topic], because [reason]. I have been [add in some credentials] and I just to work with you.

Let me know what you think and I look forward to hearing from you.

Warmly,
[your name]

When your pitch is accepted, write the post and make sure you deliver your best work. A lot of new readers and potential customers will see this, so make sure you give them your best work.

When it gets published, promote the heck out of it, show up to the post to reply to any and all comments and connect to the readers.

Giveaways & reviews. Part of building a relation with your ideal client is making sure influencers (bloggers in most cases) love your work. So set up giveaways with other bloggers, send them products to review if you have a product-based business - give them a reason to talk about your work. If they are enthusiastic about your work and products, they will talk about it on their blog, social media channels and recommend your work to their friends. That's really the best way you can get your products out there, plus you build a relationship based on trust and quality - which will be the best marketing and advertising tool you can have for your business.

Podcasts, interviews and other ways to show the person behind your brand. Same as with guest posting, it's important to get your knowledge out there. Let people see that you are there and that you know what you're talking about. Collaborating on podcasts and being interviewed are a great way to do this. You show off your personality and show that you know what you're talking about all at the same time. The other added bonus is that people will know you are a real human - which will make you much more trustworthy.

A WORD ABOUT IMAGES

What makes a good image to use with your posts or on your website? First off this depends on your business. Whatever image you use should support your brand, brand images and the overall feel of your website. If you are not sure what this is, your best bet is to start with hiring a graphic designer to help you create a style that fits your brand.

If you do know what your style is, it's much easier to pick images. So if you're a brand with a vintage feel, it's a good idea to look up images that support that. A few broad guidelines when it comes to picking images:

A strong focal point & the rule of thirds. Make sure every image you use has a strong focal point. The easier it is for the audience to spot the focal point of the images, this better balanced and more visual appealing the image will look. Another great rule to use is the rule of thirds. Divide your image into threes, both vertically and horizontally and make sure focal points are fall in one of the thirds. If you want to learn more about this you can do so here. This will strongly improve the quality of any image.

You need to like it and find it beautiful. This might seem like a simple guideline, but it's so easy to fall into the trap of picking images you think your audience wants. There is a good chance you'll end up picking images that feel like 'meh, I guess that will do.' Since you are living and breathing your brand, and in some cases, you are your brand - especially if you're selling services, this is not a smart thing to do. So make sure that you love the images when sourcing them.

It supports your articles or page on your websites. But even if you love the image, and it gives the viewer the right feeling, it still needs to support your blog post or page. It doesn't matter how much you love an image of balloons and unless you are selling balloons or hosting parties, this images will feel misplaced on your service page.

Something your readers can identify with. Lastly, think about your readers. What will resonate with them, what will inspire them, especially with the points we've just discussed in mind. Always make sure that the images fall in line with your audience. For instance, if your ideal client or readers are women between 25 and 40, it makes sense to use images featuring women in that age group, rather than men, or women in their seventies.

Different best sizes for each platform. Each platform has sweet spots when in terms of size. Instagram loves square images, long portrait images look flattering on Pinterest and Facebook loves landscape images. To help you out with the right dimensions, we've pulled together a list with some of the most popular images and their ideal sizes for each platform (as of this printing).

Facebook:
>> Cover Photo: 851 x 315
>> Profile Photo: 180 x 180
>> App Button: 111 x 74

Twitter Cover Photo: 1500 x 500

Pinterest:
>> Blog Post: 735 x 1102
>> Ideal "Pinnable Image:" 735 x 2400

Instagram – 1080x1080px

Royalty free, creative commons and other types of stock photography. You are a smart hustler, so you already know this, but there is no shame in repeating this: you cannot use a random image you find on the internet to go with your posts and on your website. Images, just as books and other creative works are licensed. Using images from the internet is there for illegal. Unless you use stock photography or images with the correct license. You have several options.

Free stock photography with Creative Commons. These images are free to use for personal or commercial use. You can find images like this on stock website such as Unsplash, Pexels, or Stocksnap.

Paid stock photography with a commercial use license. If you use images from stock photography websites such as Shutterstock, you pay so you can use the images as promotional material for you blog and business. Some stock websites are not cheap, however, there are a lot of small business owners starting their own stock photography shops especially for bloggers and small business owners. These contain less mainstream images, but are fresh and completely on trend - well worth a look!

overcoming obstacles

Memoir by Britny West

At 13 years old I hit rock bottom.

I always wondered about my father. I'd imagine what he looked like, what he smelled like, and what nicknames he would have given me had he been in my life. I wanted to know him, but I didn't even know his name and every time I asked my mom about him, the pain in her eyes made me change the topic. As I got older, I put the puzzle pieces together and figured out for myself what happened between them.

I'll never forget the day I finally got the nerve to tell my mom, "I think I know why you don't want to talk about my father." When my mom confirmed my worst fears, my world came crashing down. My mom was a rape victim and my father had been her attacker.

In that moment everything I knew to be true about myself was challenged. In an instant I felt completely unworthy and undeserving. I even felt evil. It didn't matter that my mom told me she'd go through it all over again just to have me. All I felt was deep shame for who I was and how I got here.

I look back now and wish I could hug little Britny and tell her she's more than enough. I wish I could help her feel how loved she is in that moment, but I can't. She (I) had to learn these things the hard way.

The hard way for me meant going through two miscarriages, two traumatic breakups, and chronic depression before I acknowledged my own strength, stepped out of my victimhood mentality, and realized I had the capacity to create the life I'd always wanted.

This shift happened when I had reached my breaking point with depression. I was in so much emotional pain that my only relief was the thought of ending it all. It's hard to believe I was in that space, but I was. Everything felt hopeless until I heard this loving yet firm voice in my head telling me to learn all I could about the meaning of happiness.

It sounds crazy, I know, but all of a sudden I felt like I had a purpose. I was given a life raft, and in that moment I realized more than anything I did want to live. I didn't have to be a victim of my experiences. I could choose how I wanted to feel. I could feel empowered in my story.

I consumed books and articles on happiness like it was going out of style, and I applied a lot of what I learned to my own life. I meditated, exercised, journaled, laughed, and played more. I stopped being a doormat to people who didn't value me. I stopped feeling guilty for focusing on my wants and needs.

Little by little, I began to love myself. I began to love myself more than I ever loved anyone. I didn't avert my eyes when I looked in the mirror. No, I even dared to say out loud, "I love you, Britny. I really, really love you."

My entire life changed once I took back my power. I attracted amazing friends into my life when before I struggled to connect with people. I left a company that didn't value my skills to pursue work as a health coach. As a coach, I recognized my natural ability to facilitate massive shifts in my client's mindset towards weight loss and quitting smoking. I knew there was more out there for me so I started my own coaching business helping entrepreneurs pursue their true calling and make a massive impact on the world.

Now I live a life most only dream about. I travel and live all over the world, I own a successful freedom-based business, and I'm madly in love with my boyfriend. I have this life not because I'm lucky or special or different from you. I have it, because I consciously choose empowerment every day. For me, that's happiness - acknowledging that you always have the power to feel the way you desire to feel.

Your experiences don't define you. You do.

- Britny West

Britny is a mindset coach for driven entrepreneurs ready to ditch the bullshit excuses keeping them small, own their worth, and make a massive impact on the world. Her coaching blends fierce love, kick-assery, and inspired action that helps her clients take the leading role in their life. She loves traveling so much that she sold everything she owned to become a citizen of the world. Fun fact: Everything she owns fits in one suitcase. You can find her online at www.britnywest.com.

There's going to come a day in your business when you hit your first roadblock. Maybe the first roadblock is having the courage to take the first step, or maybe you're fortunate enough to not experience a roadblock until years in. The most important thing is how you handle the obstacle and how you bounce back. What are some of the best ways to be prepared?

Have a support system. The girls of Think Creative Collective, amazing entrepreneurs like Heather Crabtree, and talented creatives like Copper Kettle Co all supported me as I made transitions and hard choices in my business and they've continued supporting me even when I've messed up! Having a support system makes things easier because you're not alone – there's someone else out there.

Know what your goals are. Why are you struggling? Why is this obstacle so significant? Know why you're so dedicated to be an entrepreneur and stand in that truth, as it will support you in the darkest days of entrepreneurship.

Be prepared. Cut back on unnecessary expenses as you transition or uplevel your business. Create space for yourself to take breaks so you don't slip into working 80-hour weeks. Understand that things will inevitably go wrong but you'll find ways to handle them.

If you're able to build a support system, understand your goals, and be prepared, surviving any obstacles that come your way throughout the entrepreneurial journey will be easier than you think!

I'M NOT A SIDE HUSTLE GAL, HOW CAN I SUPPORT PART TIME ENTREPRENEURS?

This is a question I get almost every day. Did you know that entrepreneurship isn't a new concept? In fact, the first recorded use of the word entrepreneur is in 1723 and the word itself originated from the thirteenth-century French verb *entreprendre*, meaning, "to do something."

What is new is the concept of the side hustle. As recently as 2010, running your own business part-time was not the norm. Even today, the word "side hustle" doesn't have a Wikipedia entry and no formal history can be found online. However, entrepreneurship (specifically part time entrepreneurship) is becoming the new norm. The majority of millennials (and even gen-xers) are engaged in some kind of entrepreneurial pursuit.

The reality is that entrepreneurship is becoming it's own industry. Think about it for a second – if you're a service based business, who are your clients? Many of mine are other entrepreneurs. Entrepreneurship is becoming part of the conversation as near as your kitchen table and as far as Fortune 100 boardrooms. Not everyone is ready or in a position to become an entrepreneur full time, so we choose to start a side hustle. These side hustles lend increasing credibility to the entrepreneurial industry as a whole while also providing more voices, more expertise, and more clients for each of us to learn from and work with.

As a full time entrepreneur, there are many ways you can support those working on this journey part time.

Truthfully, each of us started as some form of part time entrepreneur or "side hustler." We were college students looking for a way to make a little extra money. We were mothers and fathers who decided to turn our hobby into something that provided supplemental income. We were career professionals who wanted to be able to pay for our expensive travel hobby (ahem, that's me).

Think about "what you wish you knew back then." What mistakes did you make that might have easily been prevented with some help from a mentor? What did you spend too much time researching only to discover there was a much easier solution?

Share this knowledge with part time entrepreneurs (and each other). There's a college student or a mom out there burning the midnight oil trying to get her entrepreneurial pursuit off the ground and a piece of advice from you may be the catalyst to her achieving that goal.

MY FULL TIME JOB IS GETTING IN THE WAY

Let's think about this statement for a second. I'm a firm believer in the idea that as a Side Hustle Gal, I should love my full time job. It sounds a little backwards, I know, but follow with me for a second on this. Your full time job is your security. It provides you with healthcare, the funds to pay for the roof over your head and the food in your mouth. It gives you a sense of security that grants you the right headspace to work on your side hustle. It's a primer.

I'm not saying that having a full time job and starting a side hustle is easy – that couldn't be further from the truth. When I was getting LE Consulting off the ground, I was in college. I was going to school and bearing a 16-credit workload, working 50+ hours a week managing a McDonalds', and trying to start building a client base and doing all of the marketing and bookkeeping and everything else myself. Almost everyone who's started a business has a similar story.

Think about what life would be like without a full time job when starting a side hustle, though. Your side hustle would be your primary source of income (assuming you're single). You'd be stressed about making money first and you might not have the freedom to make decisions about your brand that are "right" instead of "necessary." You might not be able to pay for a beautiful website or a fabulous logo, because you need to eat and live and breathe. You also might even get burned out faster, because you're constantly playing catch up rather than starting out ahead.

The best part about starting your side hustle while having a full time job? It'll help you appreciate the day that your side hustle becomes your full time gig (if that's your ultimate goal). You'll be able to taste the sweetness of success and feel the overwhelming sense of accomplishment that comes from nurturing a "compensated hobby" into something that sustains you financially as well as emotionally.

time management

Memoir by Soapbox Creative Consulting

Are you exhausted? Are you having trouble thinking clearly? Are you not putting out your best work? These are just a few signs of burnout - and might I add, Side Hustle Gal, completely unnecessary and preventable signs of burnout.

There are a ton of times that I have felt like this. As an entrepreneur, I tend to overfill my plate and forget to take a day off. I forget to stop working. And most of all, I forget HOW MISERABLE IT MAKES ME. Sound familiar? It's around the 3-4 week mark when I haven't taken a break, a day to refill my well, that I notice that my mood changes, everything seems to take forever, everything is overwhelming and joyless. I am so grumpy that I can't enjoy anything and all I want to do is eat chocolate and throw myself on a couch and Netflix for hours. This is about the time when I ask myself, when was the last time I took a day off?

I have been an entrepreneur for over a decade, usually having more than one company on the go because I split myself between two industries (not recommended). And I have to tell you it's so important to take a day off. At least one day a week. If you are freaking out about this thought, it's because you are burned out and can't think straight. A day off brings so much peace to your daily routine. You think clearly. When a disturbance comes up, you can act calmly and keep your head together and the little things don't send you flying off the handle. And trust me, a peaceful mind is priceless. I know you know that because you're drooling at the thought right now.

Picture your work day, a work day where everything is in flow. All your ideas are coming to fruition, you've eaten a good breakfast, you're breathing deeply and smiling from ear to ear. You sit down to work and everything is running smooth. A client has a question. Handled. Another client?

76

Handled. Need to take a payment. Done. Need to write a blog, words start flowing like water. Inspiration is dancing with you. You write two blogs. One that you can release next week and not worry about it. This is what a free and peaceful mind can do. This is what a day off can do. Because your day off is yours to do what YOU NEED for YOURSELF. It's your time. You can stay in your pj's all day. You can meet a friend for coffee, or go for a walk, or be on a podcast. It doesn't matter. It's yours. And when you do come across a particularly stressful situation during the week, you know you have ONE DAY that you get to detach, and this is the clincher, guilt free. Your day off has to be taken guilt free. You will notice that your work is better. You are happier. And you get more done. You deserve a guilt free day off and if you don't take it, you will most likely have a guilt ridden week full of stress and overwhelm. I can't stress enough that taking a day off PAYS for itself. So go ahead. Pick a day that is your day off and do whatever the hell you want. Take your day and put up your feet. It's those days that you work so hard for, so take them before your life passes you by.

- Kat Karpoff
Kat Karpoff is the founder and creative mind behind Soapbox Creative Consulting. You can find her online at www.soapboxcreativeconsulting.com

When you're first starting out time management can seem like a daunting task. You have a lot of things going on and you just want to get on with it. Cross things off your list and move from one item to the next. Sitting down to create a planning system and routine that works just doesn't seem like your kind of thing.

But does it ever feel like you're running to catch up and never quite seem to get there? That's a very clear sign that you actually do need a planning system. And when you actually have a good system in place, you'll never have to feel like that ever again. So let's dive into time management and set you up for success.

Creating a routine. When you balance your family, full-time job and your side hustle it can feel a bit like keeping more than three balls in the air. Having a system, a routine and a set schedule can be a lifesaver. This starts with finding the time in which you do your best work. Are you a morning or an evening person? Adjust accordingly. If you're the kind of person who gets out of bed five minutes before they have to leave, getting up early to do some work won't be your kind of thing. Try setting aside some time during the evening instead after dinner or when the kids have gone to bed. Of course, the reverse is true as well. If you do your best work early in the morning, get up an hour or two earlier depending on your schedule and get to work. Not sure what is your best time? Experiment with different times and see which works best for you. And don't worry; you can always adjust later if you find it doesn't work for you.

When you know this, it's time to create a routine and some habits.

Power of habits & routine. When you have habits to support your life, it makes getting into the routine of getting things done so much easier. They say it takes 21 days to form a habit, and this really is true.

Have you ever noticed that, when you get up early in the morning during the week, you can't sleep in on the weekends? Or when you're training for a marathon. The more you do it, the easier it will feel. It's because your body is used to the rhythm: you have formed a habit.

The same goes for doing something at a specific time each day, every week. You will form a habit and a routine. The upside of this is that you don't have to think about it all that much, it will almost go automatically. And you know what's great about that? You can put your time and energy to good use and use it to get more things done because you're not wasting your time on making daily plans, or creating schedules. It's all right there in your routine. The only thing you have to think about is what you actually need to do.

Another thing that is great when creating routines and habits is to assign specific tasks to specific days. For instance: use every first Monday of the month as an admin day to make sure all your invoices and your accounting software is up-to-date. Or use every Tuesday to write your blog posts and social media updates for the week.

Start with listing all the recurring tasks you have monthly, weekly, and daily, the schedule them in and plan around it. You ensure things will get done, and your recurring tasks will never slip through the cracks again. This will create the skeleton of your daily routine.

Tools & systems. When you sit down to start working you need to know what you're going to do and what you're working on. Have a good set of planning tools and system in place is crucial here. This means always knowing when you're deadlines are when small steps of your project are due all the way to what to do with incoming email.

Especially organizing email can really eat away your time unnoticed, or how about email back and forth with a client to get them booked into your calendar.

Luckily we live in a day and age that has a lot of convenient tools for this. Such as Calendly or Acuity Scheduling for booking appointments with clients. Or even just Google Calendar where you can add people to an appointment and it shows up in their respective time zones.

We've listed some great tools to help you with in paragraph 5.3 where we will look at how tools and systems can help you reclaim your time.

Time tracking. Time tracking might seem like something you feel you won't have to do. Maybe you charge by project, or you sell paintings. You don't feel there is a point to tracking your time. However, it can really help you get some inside in what you're charging, help you plan your day and be able to give really accurate estimates to your clients.

If you feel like you never get your to-do list done in a day, this might be a sign that you're over planning on a daily basis. People seem to overestimate what they can do in a day and cram their to-lists to the brim. When you track your time, you can accurately see what you're doing and how long it's taken you. This will help you with future plannings and not to over plan at the same time.

When it comes to clients it's good to know how long a project is taking or going to take. Especially if it's on a deadline or if you use an hourly rate. This also where it's handy to know billable hours and non-billable hours.

Billable hours are the ones where you actually spend time working directly for your client, getting their work done and finishing off projects. It's the time you spend working you actually (want to) get paid for. For instance, this can be copywriting sales pages, creating a marketing plan, or in the case of a product, writing that e-book you're working on.

Non-billable hours are the opposite. It's time you work on your business doing other things. Like checking and replying to email, writing your blog posts, updating social media, etc. While all of those things are tasks that need to be done, you can't bill them to a client. However, it's crucial that you know how long these things are taking you as they will take up time in your business.

For instance, you can't work 40 hours doing work for clients and spend another 20 or 30 doing work that keeps your business running. Knowing how long other tasks will take you gives you the tools to see if you have time to take on more clients or not. It's also important that you know the balance of this so you can adjust your hourly rate accordingly. And, when your non-billable hours get too high, it might be time to consider hiring a virtual assistant to help you with this and get some time back in your schedule.

Another thing about tracking billable hours is that you can share with your client how long a task has taken you. When you're sending invoices to your clients it's great for them to know how long you spend for them working. Especially if you have an hourly contract. This way your clients can see that the time you invoice them is the time you actually worked and not the time you've spent browsing around on Facebook, or replying to your email. A great way for this is using Toggle, just hit start when you start working and stop when you go on to do something else. Easy as pie.

Say no to email and other distractions. Let's be honest here, how many times a day do you check your email? Once, twice, or do you just keep it open all day? There is no shame in admitting the latter; we've all done it one point or another. But constantly checking your email, or social media accounts for that matter, nibble away the time you have to focus on getting things done. And all those added up minutes will form a big chunk of your day.

You may or may not know that it takes your brain several minutes to completely focus on a task. Every time you pull yourself away from it by checking your email, social media or the news, your brain have to work hard to get back to the level of focus it was before the distraction. Meaning that if you completely focus on something, you'll work much more time efficient and thus get more done in the time you're actually working.

One thing that works really well is the Pomodoro Technique. This allows you to focus for 25 minutes, take a break for five minutes and get back to work for another 25 minutes. This technique is said to be the ideal attention span. Focussing for 25 minutes seems like an easy task, much better than working for a whole morning. And taking a break (ideally getting up, grabbing a drink, or visit the facilities) will help you to come back to work with fresh eyes.

You can set an alarm on your phone, or get the Chrome plugin. The plugin is amazing, as you can set it to block certain websites, so when you do drift off to open Facebook it just tells you to get back to work.

For this to work it's a good idea to put your phone in airplane mode, or better yet, put in the other room. Putting your phone away is always a good idea when it comes to getting more done - there is no temptation or sounds that indicate you need to check your messages. It really will help you get a lot done.

Balancing a social life and your side hustle. When balancing your side hustle with your social life and your day job, it can really feel like you have to keep a lot of balls in the air. Add some hobbies, sports and a love for reading in the mix and you will feel like there is never enough time in a day. What's even harder is sticking to a routine that consists of going to your day job, coming home to work on your side hustle, fall asleep and repeat the next day. This will burn you out in less than a month and that is the opposite of what you want.

That's where family and friends come in. Make sure you schedule at least two nights off per week at the bare minimum to go out and have some fun. Have a movie night with your family, have a night out with friends, go running with your running club, or have a night in and read a book - do whatever recharges your battery and leave your email and social media alone.

Actively stepping away from your side hustle and work helps you to maintain your energy levels and motivation to keep going and working when it's time to work. Stepping away and coming back to it the following day also helps you to look at things with fresh eyes and avoid a blindness to something when you've been working on it nonstop. But most of all, if your side hustle is your passion project, you need to make sure it will stay that way. And pushing yourself to work on it seven days per week even when you're tired, or want to spend time with your family is not going to keep you passionate. So schedule down time and don't be afraid to step away from it. Remember the best ideas occur when you're thinking about (and doing) something else.

Let them know. When you're starting out and you take the time to work, it will be hard for your family and friends to grasp what you're doing. Most of the time they will see that you're home and sit behind your computer. You need to communicate clearly to them what it is you're doing and let them know when you'll be working and also when you're not. This will take some time and it will be hard - trust me -, but once you let them know how they can support you, they will. In return promise them that you won't be working when you're spending time with them, you don't want to look back a year from now and realise you missed important events just because you were working.

At the same time, be flexible with your schedule, this is one of the joys of being your own boss. Say you're working three or four evenings a week, but there's a concert you really want to go to, or your kid is in a school play, or maybe there's an unexpected family visit, don't be so rigid to deny yourself this. Things that make you happy are equally as important, if not more. Things that make you happy will fuel you to keep working on your side hustle. It's all about balance and this really is an important part of that balance.

APPS & TOOLS

We've listed a few of our favorite tools and systems to help you reclaim your time starting now. They are super easy to use and most of them are free as well!

Asana. When it comes to creating to-do lists Asana gets it. You can create several different projects, tasks and you can share projects with your team (and assign members to it). You can view your to-do list with tasks assigned to you and view them in a calendar to see when tasks are due. And for the geeks amongst us, it gives you graphs that show your progress per project.

Google Calendar is a great tool for scheduling appointments. You can invite people to your appointments and it will convert automatically to their timezones. It's also great because it integrates with a lot of booking tools and software, and has a build in tasks option so you can even keep your to-do list in the same place.

Calendly & Acuity Scheduling. When booking appointments with clients, these tools will save you a lot of time. Both programs communicate with your calendar (like Google!) and the availability you've chosen. Your (future) client is able to pick the day and date that suits them best and the program will automatically add them to your calendar. Best thing? It even allows you to add a questionnaire your clients need to fill out before your appointment and it sends your client reminders - talk about saving time!

Trello. This is a to-do list system that allows you to drag and drop tasks through a timeline. This is especially useful if you have tasks that follow a certain timeline. It's also a great tool when you work with a team you want to check on the status of certain elements of a project.

17hats. As business owners, you have a lot of different aspects to running your business. Sometimes it can feel like you have to be everywhere at the same time and wear a lot of different hats. 17hats is doing that for you, combining all the aspects of your business in one handy tool so you'll always have everything in one place - and save you a lot of time in the process.

Toggle. A great handy tool for time tracking. You can use it as a desktop version or as an app on your phone. You can create several different projects and tag them to clients. You can even add if the time worked is billable or not. Big plus: it gives you a weekly overview so you can see at a glance how you've spent your week.

CoSchedule. The best thing about CoSchedule is that you can connect it to your self hosted Wordpress account and your social media all at the same time. When you're planning your posts you'll write your social media updates at the same time. CoSchedule will plan them in for you at the time you've assigned and you won't have to worry about remembering to post to social media anymore. And if you're connected to Buffer? Good news the two work together pretty well.

Edgar / Hootsuite. Managing several social media accounts and tired of switching? These tools make it easy to schedule, post and manage several social media accounts in one place. It also gives you a bunch of great analytics so you always know what works and what didn't. No more guesswork and more time efficient.

Buffer. This is a one-stop shop for social media. It allows you to post to your Twitter account, but also on your personal Facebook, your Facebook pages and in your Facebook groups. It doesn't stop there, though, you can also use Buffer to posts to LinkedIn, Google+ and Pinterest. Buffer helps you determine the ideal schedule for your posts and shows them to you on a calendar.

Tailwind. This is a social media scheduling tool, especially for Pinterest. It allows you to easily add a pin to several different boards and creates a custom schedule so you'll always make the most of your pins. It's easy to add descriptions, tags, and link backs to the original posts.

Evernote. You can use Evernote for literally anything. Creating content, saving important information, using it as a to-do list, you name it! You can use the desktop version of Evernote, as well as the app. You will always have the latest version of your notes on hand as Evernote stores everything in the cloud. You can save notes, sort them in folders (notebooks), or tag the. The entire program is created to create, store and find information quickly.

Hello Sign. If you're working with clients and creating contracts this tool is amazing for quickly signing them digitally. Gone are the days where you have to print contracts, sign them, scan them and attach them to an email. Now you can sign contracts in a few clicks.

Strict Workflow. Love the Pomodoro technique? This Google Chrome plugin is a shiny red tomato in the corner of your browser. You click it to activate your 25 minutes of work. Before you start you can add the websites you want to block so you can't access them during your 25 minutes (if you try, it just tells you to go back to work). After that time your alarm goes off, and you get a green tomato and five minutes of free time before you head into your next round of work.

Stay Focused. Similar to Strict Workflow, you can add website to this app to block during your time of undisturbed work. However you can use this Chrome app in several different ways. You can either use it to block the entire internet, or you can use it to run in the background and set yourself a limit of 'distracting website time' per day. The nuclear option is particularly good, as it blocks every website in Chrome, but you can still keep your connection for things like Spotify or Evernote.

reach: a step in
the right direction

I landed my first client, now what?

Memoir by Reid & Brittany Photography

I'm biting the bullet and writing this because I can't find one blog or one person to say what I want to tell you and it's way too important to stay quiet. Somewhere, there has to be at least one person who is desperately searching for the answer like I have been for years now. There has to be somebody like me who has spent hours watching videos, reading blogs, going to workshops and conferences, trying to find someone who is in the same unique shoes. We all want to find someone who understands us, right?

What is Hustle? *When I say "Hustle," what immediately comes to mind? Coffee? Messy buns? The word printed in a cute gold font on a white t-shirt, coffee mug, or canvas? Now take a second and think of what hustle looks like practically in your life. I'm talking to you, 8-5 day job-worker who has a husband and maybe some kids and pets, and parents and siblings, and a home that requires occasional cleaning and extra-curricular commitments and a human body that will only let you function if you feed it the right things and let it sleep for 8 hours a night... and running a creative business "on the side."*

Am I getting warm? "Just drink more coffee" doesn't work for you like your Instagram buddies, because they must be superhuman and don't feel the side effects of overdosing on caffeine. Or maybe they do, and just don't let the Instaworld know when they go into a coma of exhaustion. When you stay up too late and wake up too early a few days in a row, you start falling asleep at your day job, and sure as heck don't have the energy or mental ability to give your business and your loved ones the time of day when you get home. You know what happens next, don't you? The guilt sets in for neglecting your family. Your spouse says they miss you and your kids ask you why you won't play with them. No one has clean clothes to wear, and the dishes in the sink are starting to resemble Mount Vesuvius as they spill out onto the counter.

You feel torn. Your family needs you. Your business needs you. You need you. You've read so many blogs, listened to so many webinars (because who has time to actually sit and watch something for an hour and a half?) and paid so much for in-person education that you can't imagine deviating from the plan. If you don't follow their advice, the things that made them successful, you'll never get there. You will never grow enough to quit your soul-sucking day job. You won't book as many weddings, as many sessions, get more Instagram followers, Facebook likes or blog comments. Your clientele will slowly disappear and your followers will stop following. People won't respect you, care about your work, or want to invest their money in you. So you tell your husband and kids that you just need to finish this last blog then you'll spend time with them. Just one last session to edit. Just one more Facebook post to schedule. Just a couple of emails. But just… never ends.

There are hundreds, maybe thousands, of sources of education that teach "hustle." Day job, night job, no job… just keep hustling and doing all of the right things and it will pay off. Your hard work and talent will pay off and you can live your dream full time. What if that's not the case? Hustling and doing all of the right things is growing your business, but much slower than you hoped, and ruining your family in the process. And your health. What now? Easy answer: make more time for family and don't put your business first anymore. Find balance and create margin. Okay, but what does that look like practically? Where is part 2 of that webinar? How do you prioritize better, and still do it all? I've been asking that questions for years now.

Are you ready for the answer?

You DON'T do it all. If you're a control freak like me, you need to take a deep breath right now. Good? Now let me say it again: you don't. Do. It. All. No, I'm not talking about outsourcing. Don't get me wrong, outsourcing is an incredible solution for busy business owners, and has transformed the lives of many of our good friends. But if you are working your tail off to grow a business that is nowhere close to paying you enough to put a roof over your family's head, feed them, keep the electricity turned on and gas in the car, outsourcing isn't an option. Let's not forget about making payments toward the debt you incurred trying to get the business started in the first place. When outsourcing isn't an option, what is?

What I finally learned, after fighting the system for years and feeling completely helpless and alone, is that maybe hustle isn't about doing it all, all of the time. Sacrificing my marriage for consistent blogging and social media presence. Poisoning myself with large amounts of sugar and caffeine to turn around a wedding in a week, so they'll be impressed and refer their friends. Maybe the hustle is actually about saying the hardest word in an entrepreneur's vocabulary: "No." Or, "Wait." For workaholics like you and me, that type of hustle is far more difficult than the typical definition.

***Real Hustle.** In Jon Acuff's book, Do Over, he says that hustle has seasons. Hustle looks different for every individual, in every season. A mother of a 3-month-old who is returning to work after maternity leave does not need to be blogging, editing, Instagramming, and Facebooking every weekday, shooting weddings and sessions on the weekend, and then adding in designing a new pricing guide. That is not her season. When you're falling asleep at your day job because you've barely slept all week and your employer is starting to notice- that is not your season. But don't worry, seasons don't last forever.*

Reid and I are a team in this business. There are two people to divide the work. So we shouldn't have a problem with this, right? Again, one size does not fit all. Husband and wife teams are not all created equal. Having two people doesn't mean that we are both gifted at all of the tasks involved in our business, and that the workload is 50/50. For the longest time, I thought that we were doing it wrong, and all of the other husband/wife teams MUST be doing it "right." After learning the long way, I've finally accepted the truth about hustle. Hustle for me is knowing when to let it go, when to say no, and when to wait.

***The Turning Point.** It was late Sunday night and Reid somberly walked in to the office. I knew what was coming and I grew irritated. We had been really busy* *for the past couple of weeks and unable to spend much, if any, quality time together. Another workweek was about to begin, and he just wanted some time with his wife without the glow of the laptop screen on her face. I blogged faithfully every Monday, Wednesday and Friday and was NOT about to mess that up. If I missed a Monday, what would people think of us as business owners? If we missed a Monday, how could we be trusted? No one would want to hire us! We began to argue again about my inability to ever stop working, and then my husband said it. The words that changed everything. As I sat there in my desk chair, with my "Marriage Monday" blog (oh, the irony) waiting to be written, my husband told me that he wished I cared about him as much as I did about the business. GUT PUNCH. There I was, trying to write marriage advice while I was destroying my own.*

The Fix. *Is consistent blogging an incredible business tool, and an effective way to make a personal connection with your present and future clients? Absolutely, and it was one that I refused to relinquish. We just couldn't afford not to! On top of that, I was spending time each day designing a 24-page pricing guide in Photoshop (with zero prior Photoshop experience)! Something had to go. What I learned is that the cost of saying no to my husband and health was far greater than the cost of saying no to blogging 3+ times per week. I decided that during this season, I would only blog sessions, weddings and the occasional personal post, and would work on the pricing guide as I was able. And guess what happened...we kept booking weddings. Not only that, but we booked almost as many weddings in a 3 month period than the total* *number of weddings we shot in the entire year of 2015! We get inquires more consistently now than we ever have! Our business did not cease to exist because we didn't follow the proven plan of success. I truly believe that God has blessed our business because we put our marriage back where it belongs.*

__New Seasons.__ How do you know when the season changes, and it's safe and wise to add something back to your plate? I think this looks different for everyone but there is one question that applies to everyone. "If I say yes to this, will I have to say no to something else?" If the answer is yes, then you need to evaluate your options carefully, and determine the value of the task in question. Don't believe that because it's not the right time to say yes that you have to say no. Be patient, be wise, and give yourself grace. You can't, and don't have to do it all. By saying yes to blogging 3+ times a week, and working on the pricing guide daily, I was saying no to my husband. At this point in our business, we believed that creating a product which would better educate our potential clients on the front end on who we are and our process was crucial to our growth and their experience with us. We evaluated the options, and decided what was more important at that time. By saying no/wait to the blogging, and yes to putting our marriage first, we hustled. By saying no, we were blessed exponentially.

__What's Next?__ Odds are that you've heard a lot of this before. You can't do it all, your life and business need margin, keep your priorities in line, etc. etc. Have you stopped to consider whether you truly believe it? Slow and steady wins the race and everybody wrecks on the *fast track. The downside to the plethora of available education these days is that it is SO easy to let yourself believe that the only way to be truly successful is to follow ALL of the advice. It can be detrimentally blinding and suck the joy right out of you to want so desperately to be full time, to book destination weddings, to be busier than the other guy, to make more and work less. I can say that with full confidence because that is something we deal with on a daily basis. Social media can make you feel like a failure, simply because there are hundreds of people that are in the shoes you want to wear. Please, please don't let it suck you in. Please don't let it hold you there. Take their advice with a grain of salt. Soak up all of the education you can, but ultimately you have to do what works for you. What works for your situation, your season and your family, in your market, and define what success is to you. Don't allow others to define it for you.*

- Brittany Riggan
Alongside her husband Reid, Brittany is the founder of Reid & Brittany Photography. You can find her online at www.reidandbrittany.com

Your first client will be the one you never forget. Many business owners save the first dollar they make – be sure to do something similar to commemorate this amazing step towards a bountiful and successful business.

Your first client will also probably be your worst. If you're anything like me, your first client will show you all the holes in your business – missing parts of your contract, broken parts of your process, and things you need to improve on or learn more about. My first tip? Use a blank piece of paper to track all of the "a-ha" moments you experience throughout working with your first client.

To save you some heartache and strife as you take on your first client, here's the process I use to acquire and onboard clients. Hopefully it will help you too!

STEP ONE: THE INQUIRY

This is before you've landed a client. They've found you on social media, from your blog, or even from a referral. You want to make sure your intake form helps answer many of the questions you'll need to ask to help them select a package and identify whether or not you can help them.

Inquiry Form Questions:
1. First Name / Last Name
2. Email Address
3. Package of Interest (if applicable)
4. Business Name (if applicable)
5. Website (if applicable)
6. Why they need your help (i.e. what are they struggling with, what type of photos do they want, what kind of wedding are they having)
7. How did they find you.

That last question – how did they find you – is so important. It'll help you track what your best referral sources are!

Once you receive the inquiry, you'll want to reply with a warm introductory email asking them when they'd be available to connect (preferably with your scheduler link to reduce back and forth), a general overview of your process, and answers to any questions they might have asked.

"use a blank paper to track a-ha moments."

STEP TWO: THE CONSULTATION

Depending on your business process and type, you'll want to decide on either an in-person or virtual consultation. This is the time to chat through their answer to "why they need your help" from your inquiry form. You'll want to hear them out, offer suggestions, verify whether or not you'll be able to help, and outline next steps.

STEP THREE: SUMMARY AND SIGN

I call this step "summary and sign" because it makes for a smooth transition from "here's the information from our consultation" to "here's a quote and contract for you to review and sign." You'll want to do this through your client management software – in my case, I send the proposal (aka quote) and contract through HoneyBook and include the call notes in the email that has the link to those items.

STEP FOUR: AGREEMENT

This is the step where the client reviews and signs your contract and pays your deposit/retainer fee. Simple! This step should automatically trigger the sending of a "new client onboarding" email to whoever is responsible for getting the client set up on your processes, any project management software, etc.

STEP FIVE: NEW CLIENT

You'll want to send along a thank you card (and gift if appropriate) to the client to welcome them to your business family. You or someone on your team will want to add the client to any project management software, ensure a workflow has been initiated, and send along a welcome packet. My welcome packet includes the following:

1. "Next Steps" Checklist – an outline of what the process looks like and what the client needs to do during each phase.
2. Tools for Success document – resources for using any of the tools I use with the client (i.e. Trello).
3. LE Consulting Policies and Processes document (usually contained in the contract, sometimes sent separately as a reminder – this includes communication policies, expectations, etc.).

I then schedule a kick-off call and the client's project officially begins!

STEP SIX: WORK ON THE PROJECT

Depending on what industry you're in, this phase may take two weeks, one month, six months, or even more than a year. It's critical that you keep track of where you're at in your process and make sure the client knows too. Your clients will appreciate not having to ask you where things are at and what to expect next.

STEP SEVEN: PROJECT CLOSE-OUT

At this point, your project with the client is pretty much over. You'll want to hold a wrap-up meeting (or send a wrap-up email). This is also the time to ask for reviews as well as celebrate your client on social – they'll appreciate the public shout out! It's also the time to send one more thank you card as well as a gift, if that is part of your process.

Following a consistent process each time you work with a new client will ensure that all of your clients receive the same level of quality service that you want to be known for. Outlining your process (or using mine and tweaking it to suit your needs) will help ensure that you don't forget any steps or miss any parts of what you want to accomplish.

If you want to learn more about having a good client process, there are two excellent e-courses I'd recommend:

Heather Crabtree's Streamline with Systems
Courtney Johnson's Yay for Clients

Both of these courses are great for setting up, adhering to, and tweaking (as needed) business-specific and client-specific processes and procedures.

client-creator relationship

Memoir by Emily Walker

Some of my favorite memories are from college. However, everything wasn't always a bucket of roses, as they say. We have either been there ourselves or have known someone who has felt the lint in their pocket while being a full-time student. This was so me! Countless hours of class work coupled with working multiple jobs left me thinking there had to be some way I could earn cash without having to go to another job. This was when I became a Side Hustle Gal.

I interviewed and became a fashion merchandiser for a fabulous jewelry company out of NYC. While this was not an endeavor I entirely started on my own (hint: your side hustle doesn't have to be!), it was an opportunity to cultivate my own personal business and clientele. I would no longer have to trade time for money but instead would run an online boutique where people could shop whether I was working or not! Oh but wait, clients? I would probably need some of those.

The first year was tough. Many of my first sales came from the support of friends and family. It took time to establish myself in the brand I represented and to build a base of repeat customers. I booked pop-up events, planned marketing campaigns, started a Facebook page, and so much more. Through it all I have found that consistency is key! Are you being consistent?

I often check in with myself and ask: Am I timely in correspondence? Am I consistently placing orders when necessary, following up, booking vendor events, posting to social media, and processing returns? What are you doing to provide consistency, or what could you implement to get you there? When you are consistent in your business, you gain a reliable reputation. Clients are more likely to stick with a brand they can depend on!

In the first year of my side hustle, and today just the same, it has been important to not only be consistent, but to go above and beyond in being personable and genuine to my customers. I always want them to know they are appreciated and valued! Send personal thank you cards/emails, and take the time to get to know them. Who are your customers? Are you present to support them? What are they passionate about

As an entrepreneur running your side hustle, you are your brand. Create brand fanatics that will spread the word about your business for you! There is always going to be competition. Go the extra mile to exceed customer expectations so they come back to YOU. What does this look like in your business?

Your customers will see the passion you possess. Keep your fire and momentum going! Your side hustle is exciting! Believe in your brand, take the time and put in the work to grow your customer base, develop customer trust through consistency, invest in customer appreciation, and cultivate customer relationships. No one is going to put into your business what you are not willing to invest yourself. Best of luck to you!

- Emily Walker

Along with her full-time job as a retail manager and stylist, Emily Walker side hustles as a fashion merchandiser and brand representative of Chloe + Isabel, an innovative and fashionable jewelry lifestyle brand out of NYC. Check out Emily's online boutique at www.chloeandisabel.com/boutique/emilywalker

Working *with* your clients is an incredibly important part of growing your business. Being their friend, however, is a whole different story.

Don't get me wrong, I love building awesome relationships with incredible entrepreneurs as I work through my business. However, becoming "best friends" with my clients has been a surefire route to sticky situations in business. How do you keep things separated? Here are my best tips:

Don't friend your clients on Facebook. I don't know about you, but I only have 75 friends on Facebook. I know, as a millennial that seems almost crazy, but it's completely true. I love knowing that I can post whatever I want on Facebook and only a handful of people are going to see it. You don't want to have to worry about posting about your basement flooding and all of your clients seeing the photos, because you probably shouldn't friend your clients on Facebook until their project is over. How do I handle declining friend requests that come from clients? I have a "template message" saved in my Notes app that I copy-paste and tweak as needed for clients and business connections that I don't feel close enough with to share my Facebook life with. Here's a sample you can use:

Hi [Potential Facebook Friend]!
Thank you so much for sending me a friend request! It means a lot to me that you value our relationship and would like to stay connected. I just wanted to stop by and say that I keep my personal Facebook page pretty private – I'm sure you can understand. However, I'd love to connect with you! Feel free to head over to facebook.com/[yourbizpage] and hit "Like" or send me an email at [yourbizemail] and we can stay connected.
All my best, [Your Name]

I just copy-paste a message similar to that, tweak for a personal touch, and send to the person that added me via Facebook message. I haven't had any issues so far!

Don't let your clients text you. Unless you're super into texting, I'm sure getting texts from clients can be frustrating, especially if they're texting you when you're on a date, out with friends, or even on vacation! I've worked hard to train my clients to not text me unless it is an absolute emergency and so far it's working well. If I do get a text from a client that is not emergent, I send them an email that contains my reply to their text (assuming it's within my business hours) and gently remind them that all written communication should be via email for ease of organization.

Have set office hours. If you're managing a lot of clients, it's important to have set office hours. These are the hours that your clients can expect near-immediate responses from you via email or schedule phone calls with you. These hours do not represent all the hours you'll be working but they do represent the hours during which you're checking email. This is important to do, because otherwise you could very well spend your whole week answering emails and taking phone calls! If you need to set (or change) your hours, send a "client update" email with all the information contained within. By doing this, you can be sure that all of your clients will receive the update and are now aware of your new hours. Another tip? Put them in your email signature! I keep my office hours in my email signature because it's a daily reminder to clients of when I'm available and it's easy for them to just check any email from me to see what those hours are.

Have a standard procedure for revisions and changes. You'll want to document any requested revisions or changes to the work product you're providing your client and you'll want to be able to reference it later if you have any issues. Having a set process for clients to submit revisions will be key to managing this with ease. My favorite method to get revisions? I request an email with numbered edits and a scanned or edited PDF of the original with the numbers assigned to the elements in question. It makes the edit process go by so much more quickly and the client is able to be more clear on what it is she needs changed or corrected.

Make a list of your ideas for peaceful
client relationship management below:

Three cheers to feeling more confident in your client relationships and interactions!

taxes and money

Memoir by Copper Kettle Co.

Accounting is not a sexy topic. Even John Grisham, the guy who writes books about lawyers, doesn't write very often or at all about accounting. Despite its decided non-sexiness, accounting is ubiquitous, and why shouldn't it be? It is about simply knowing where your money is and where it's going. If you run a business, you should know where every dollar goes.

The sooner you come to love accounting, the sooner your business will flourish. Of course your business won't flourish if all you know is accounting (unless you're an accountant) but it is a necessary condition to success. That's probably another reason nobody likes accounting. It feels like homework... in school. You don't get paid for it, but not doing it hinders your progress.

However, I'm here to tell you that accounting can provide you with some incredibly useful information! I'll tell you a fun (not!) story about how accounting could have prevented catastrophe and then we can all go to happy hour in our respective cities, mission accomplished.

Accounting can tell you things that your bank account cannot. For example, it's possible, due to timing issues, for you to be incredibly in debt when it feels like you're flush with cash.

Have you ever had one of those months where you feel like you're doing great and you have all sorts of money and where did all this money come from? Because we have. Not often enough to actually be wealthy, but often enough to know the feeling. We start feeling a little too proud. We think to ourselves, "I knew that hard work would pay off. Oh hey there, friends and acquaintances who (I imagine) thought I wouldn't be successful." So we go out to dinner a few too many times and bask in the glory of our great prosperity, positive that we've turned the corner this time and we'll never have to cut it close with bills again! And then you realize that you didn't pay the mortgage last month. And the mortgage is due again next week.

Shit.

Thaaaat's why it felt like we had money.

I know what you're thinking, "Tell me please, do you have a boring business administration related tool that could have prevented this tragedy?" Absolutely I do! Accounting could have prevented this tragedy. If you kept a set of books for your personal life, you would know that you still owed the bank a whole ton of money, and that as your bank balance climbed to a couple thousand dollars, the amount of cash that was actually yours was actually only approaching zero from the red side.

I'm not going to tell you that you should keep books for your personal life; I'm trying to improve your life, not bury you in a sea of red ink and calculator tape. But if you're a small business owner, then keeping a solid set of books for your business will feel a lot like keeping a set of books for your personal life.

Unglamorous as it may be, accounting can mean the difference between staying in business and going back

116

to work for the man, which we're all studiously trying to avoid. So the rule that we learned from our poor friend who can't pay his mortgage is that profit has to take into account money you are owed as well as money that you owe people! Cash isn't always a reliable indicator of the health of a business. Before you call me a genius, let me tell you that someone, somewhere, thought of this sometime ago.

It's called accrual accounting, and it's very useful in certain circumstances, specifically where I.O.Us (to or from you) account for a large portion of your business. I know it sounds trivially easy to grasp, but I worked as an accountant for several years, and there was a constant stream of clients that confused cash flow for profitability.

Distilled to its most primitive form, accrual accounting is taking adding up all the money you collected, subtracting the money you spent, and then adding the money that is owed to you, and subtracting the money that is owed by you.

And it's important that it all happens in the same time period. Don't add in all the money people owe you for the 3 months of work you have booked, and then only subtract out one month of credit card payments.

You'll be in great shape once you can do this in your head over different time periods. I never trust my bank account. Instead, I think about what bills haven't been paid for the month and who still owes us money by the end of the month. The difference, plus what's in the bank, is how much money we actually have on a very short-term basis. To get the real picture, I have to subtract the mortgage and the student loans, which makes the number depressingly negative.

Of course there are whole books written about accrual accounting and whole careers to be made from deciding when to record revenue and expenses. It can get very technical, but at the simplest level, it's about getting a more accurate picture of your financial situation. And you don't have to be perfect at it either! But it's important to start thinking in accrual terms as your business grows so that you don't get caught off guard when the amounts get bigger and the time periods get longer.

Understanding your finances can be the difference between success and failure for a business. It can mean a stronger negotiating position when you're trying to get a lease or a loan. It can also mean you're better informed when considering the cost of marketing or purchasing new technology.

As your understanding of accounting increases, decisions that were once agonizing will become a snap, and new opportunities will seem to magically appear, as you are able to make the numbers work. Turns out accounting isn't that boring at all! (Ok, yes it is, but at least it's kind of useful, and very important to small business owners such as yourself.)

- *Kelly Sherwood*

Kelly makes up one half of the Copper Kettle Co. team (and wrote their contribution here) and Kyrsten is our cover designer! Ever since she'd had opportunities to organize and arrange projects, Kyrsten was on it. She's pretty much a natural-born entrepreneur!

Kelly's way more fancy than Kyrsten is (or so she says), with his University of Washington Law School degree, 99th percentile SAT score, 95th percentile LSAT score, etc. WOAH! You can find them over at www.ckc.io.

Fun fact: when I was a senior in college, I worked for HR Block full-time. In fact, I even worked there for two years after I finished undergrad, just because the part time money was so good (your hourly rate was dependent on your previous year's profitability – meaning the maximum hourly rate was limitless!).

Even if you don't have a basic foundation in taxes, or even a more advanced one like Kelly, there are a few business basics that you can rely on to keep your financial house in order. Follow along below and make some notes!

Take a moment to learn the basics. Educating yourself about the various aspects of finance (regardless of existing skill level) is a great way to ground yourself as well as to have a level of knowledge to understand what your bookkeeper or accountant might be doing for you. Reading financial statements is also an excellent skill to have, even in your own personal life.

Set a business budget. Determine what the critical needs are for your business and set a budget for expenditures. Project how much you'll make in business based on history (whether you have a couple years of business finances to look at or just a couple days). What makes my business budget? Take a peek at a few of the categories I track:

INCOME:

- Services rendered
- Affiliate income
- Passive revenue streams
- Sale of assets

EXPENSES:

- Advertising

- Marketing materials (printed – like business cards – and digital – like my website)
- Business Maintenance
- Office Supplies
- Client expenses

Creating a chart of accounts will be important for you to report expenses vs. income and further break down where your money comes from and where it gets spent.

Track everything. Whether you use an excel spreadsheet, QuickBooks Online, or you pay a bookkeeper, it's critical that you track every dollar that enters and exits your business. Having a separate business bank account is also critical for good business practices. My favorite is Bank of America. As of this printing, if you spend more than $250 a month using your debit card, there are no fees to have a business account with them.

Manage expenses. Be realistic. Regardless of whether you're the owner of a new or seasoned business, being savvy with your money is a great thing. Use open source or free software when possible, check out free services for video conferences and other calls, even using inexpensive vs. high end solutions is a smart business move.

Cloud-Based Accounting Software is worth it. Using a cloud-based software is a huge convenience as a busy business owner. Being able to sneak a peek at your finances on the road, in the air, or even down the street is a great advantage.

Know where you're at. Take the time to check in on your business finances. Know how profitable you are, have an expectation of whether or not your business will grow this quarter, and be able to share that story as appropriate. Set aside just 15 minutes a week to organize your finances, and don't let other things take priority during this time. It might sound painful, but you'll be able to see into your business better which will enable to you make more informed financial decisions. This will also help you be more relaxed come tax time.

Don't forget about the people. It doesn't matter if you're the only person on the payroll or if you pay thousands. You'll want to track how much you spend on paying the people that make your business go. If it's just you, this will help you figure out whether you can afford to pay yourself a bonus. If there are multiple people involved, it'll help you figure out if you are maximizing your people's time and talents.

Don't forget to get paid. Sounds silly, right? But if you're not tracking your invoices, how do you know whether or not you've been paid for all of them. You could be collecting payments late, or missing some altogether. Make sure you're properly tracking all payments due and recording when each invoice is paid, how long customers generally take to pay, and which customers you've had difficulties collecting payments from in the past.

Make some notes to help you get your financial house in order:

grow: onward
and upward we go

business maintenance

Memoir by Maggie Giele

I fell into marketing almost accidentally. I've always been fascinated with psychology and why people make decisions, and did a Master's in Science in Marketing, mostly because it seemed like a good idea at the time. My degree was tough and focused on statistics, data analysis and market research, not even close to the psychology I was fascinated by. It was disappointing. At the very least, I was calmed by the idea that such a degree was supposed to open doors to a great career path.

I spent six months after graduation applying for jobs. Crickets. A fresh graduate, and a new country with a new language, with a marketing degree in the financial capital of Europe. Great combination. Plus, I was constantly hearing this perspective of marketing:

"Oh, you're in marketing?" the suit in front of me smirked. "So, like choosing colours"

There was a constant battle. Every networking event, every time I met someone new, and they found out I did marketing, I got the same kind of responses – it was vague, fluffy and manipulative. Worst were the responses that companies – big and small - didn't even need marketing departments. It was just a suck on time and money.

Marketing was treated with the same kind of disdain found with second-hand car salesmen (who have an incredibly tough job) and Wall Street bankers (let's not go there).

I rebelled against this. I hated the idea of manipulation, and with all these conversations, started doubting what marketing was and why I actually wanted to do it. This is what I wanted people to know about marketing. It works. And – done well – it's not manipulative, or sleazy, or underhanded. I started learning how to code websites. The reason was very simple – I was getting desperate for that corporate job I wanted, and thought that adding a more 'tangible' skill to my resume would help me in getting some interviews.

A friend of a friend found out I was playing around with websites, and hired me to make one. Then someone else hired me. Then another. Suddenly, I realised I was a freelancer web designer – something I fell into by pure accident.

I also realised another thing. While designing and creating websites for my clients, I was helping them with their marketing and business strategies. One client hit his highest month of revenue of the year right after we worked together – and his website wasn't even up yet. Seeing these actual, tangible results gave me the confidence to launch the business I had always wanted. Helping business owners and entrepreneurs build businesses worth celebrating through business and marketing strategy.

Marketing is about getting the right products and services, in front of the right people, in the right way, at the right time. It's about attracting your audience to you so that you can help solve their problems, through your product or service.

You can have the most amazing business, product or service on offer, but if your marketing isn't done right – if the relevant people, those who need what you have, and want it, don't know about it…well, then you don't have much of a business, and you're definitely not able to help the people you want to help.

- Maggie Giele
Maggie Giele, MSc. is a digital strategist. She and her team help success-driven business owners build businesses worth celebrating through online marketing and business strategy. You can find her online at @MaggieGiele.

One of my favorite ways to encourage someone to try a little business maintenance is to start by planning out their social media and blog content at least a month in advance. Why plan social media / blog content 1+ month in advance? This allows you to have a consistency, rhythm, and cohesiveness to your content. You don't want to blog about "social media management" one month and then blog about "Pinterest management" the next! You'd want to do a month dedicated to social media management and then break it out by platform and do a post (or more) a week on each platform. Planning content in advance lets you see opportunities for deeper and more thoughtful content.

Once you systemize your social media, you'll also want to check that it works. Ignore a growth in social media followership and try looking at engagement.

What is engagement? Engagement at its purest form is the number and types of interactions your account receives on content you share. For Instagram, this means the number of likes and comments your photos garner. Regrams apply as well, but they are much harder to track, so they have been excluded for the purpose of this explanation.

How do i calculate engagement? An incredibly simple way to calculate engagement is to look at your past nine photos on Instagram. Total up all the likes and comments across the photos, then divide the total number by nine. Take that number and divide it by your total number of followers. The result is a rate of engagement that you can then track, monitor, and share. For example:

Izzy Instagrammer has 12,956 followers. Across her most recent nine photos, she received a total of 4,500 likes and/or comments. 4,500/9 = 500. Her average of 500 "engagements" per post is then divided by her total followers (12,956) to get a result of 0.0385, or 38.5%.

She then makes a note of 38.5% as today's engagement rate. She can track this rate going forward by doing the same calculation as often as she likes so that she can gauge increases and decreases in engagement, shift her Instagram strategy, and even report this number to potential media partners.

How do I benchmark engagement? As a benchmark, the average "per follower" engagement rate is 4.21% on posts by top brands for Instagram (and this engagement rate is 58x higher than Facebook and 120x higher than Twitter using the same formula). Comparing on a percentage basis is the best way to look at your own engagement vs. competitors, as they may have more or less followers than you. (For example, Red Bull has 4.3M Instagram followers and shows a 1.7% engagement rate. Izzy Instagrammer has about 13k followers but shows a 38.5% engagement rate.) This comparison method allows you to disregard the follower "numbers" and look at the quality of your followers as compared to your competitors. Your goal should be to have a higher engagement rate than your followers.

TRAVELING AS AN ENTREPRENEUR

Traveling as an entrepreneur can be exciting but it can also be incredibly stressful. Here are three key ways to make it a little bit easier for you and your clients.

Managing Clients. There are two different ways to manage clients while you're traveling. I tend to choose one or the other based on the type of travel I'm headed on.

Method 1: The "I'm out of town" method. It's okay to take time away from your business, just like employees take time away from the corporate world. To do this best, you'll want to make sure your clients are aware that you'll be on vacation. It's up to you whether you check in for emergencies only or completely unplug, but you'll want your clients to know. If you have a VA or other assistant, consider asking them to cover down for you while you're gone. Then, when you're on vacation, make sure you actually take the time to unplug.

Method 2: Sometimes, Method 1 just doesn't work, and that's okay too. Method 2 is to check in on a limited basis. Work for maybe 2-3 hours a day. It's important to note that you are on vacation so you do need to take some time for yourself, but checking in is okay too. Set up some parameters and stick to them. You and your clients will both appreciate it!

Business Travel. Traveling for business can be a lot of fun. There are a few ways you can make it more enjoyable. First, register with GOES so that you can get Global Entry and a known traveler number. Next, fly with carry-on luggage only, even internationally (see below for my favorite company). Doing this means you'll get everywhere faster and you'll lessen your risk of lost luggage! Finally, take advantage of any perks you might have because of your credit card companies - including access to airport lounges, discounts on WiFi on the airplane, and so much more!

Basic Travel Tips. When traveling (whether domestically or abroad), there are certain steps you can take to make things go smoothly (even if you're not traveling for business). Here are my favorites:

As a frequent business and leisure traveler, one of the worst parts of traveling for me is always baggage claim and security. To help alleviate these things, I've started traveling much lighter than I used to. I have a carry on bag from Away Travel that includes a phone charger in the bag itself, as well as a laundry bag and a compression divider, so I have everything in one place.

When I do pack, I pack 100% neutral colors—they tend to look classier (especially when traveling through Europe) and they mix and match well (so I pack less clothes). I also don't pack toiletries (unless traveling to a more remote location) because the hotels and AirBNBs I stay in typically provide these items.

A REVOLUTIONARY IDEA:
START A BUSINESS WITH JUST $0.10

Entrepreneurship can be expensive but it is just as easy to start a business with just ten cents in your pocket. It's important to note that this is primarily true for service-based businesses, but even a lemonade stand can be started for less than ten cents.

How do you start a business for less than ten cents? Give this method a try.

1. Start by networking. Join entrepreneur groups on Facebook, attend in-person networking events, etc. Share your knowledge freely and cultivate respect as someone who has important knowledge and skills to impart on others.

2. Start an email list. Send an email to the people you've cultivated relationships with and ask them if they'd like to receive a weekly newsletter with similar tips and knowledge to what you've already shared. Add the people who respond "yes" to your email list (MailChimp is a free service for your first 2,000 subscribers – this is a good place to start).

3. After you've sent the email list for a few weeks, create an email series (ideally a five day course) that imparts actionable knowledge on how to resolve a pain point you've noticed among your readers. For example, if your readers have trouble figuring out how to grow their team and you have experience in hiring

and managing people, write a five-day email course on hiring and managing people.

4. Send an email to your email list and invite them to join the course. You can price it however you'd like but a good price is $24 or $49 to start. Add those who sign up to a group within your email list and set up the five-day email course to send to that group.

5. If you've sold the course to 2 or 4 people (depending on your pricing), you've earned enough money to build a website. Head on over to Squarespace and build a website that
   a. Lists the other services you'll offer with descriptions
   b. Has an about page that explains your credentials, background, and who you are
   c. Has a blog where you can continue sharing free knowledge with others
   d. Has a place for people to contact you to hire you for these services

As you can see, this business model requires some legwork to get it started, but it is founded without any capital input on your end apart from time and knowledge. As you enter the website and services phase of your business, you're in a better place than most new entrepreneurs, because you already have an email list and an audience that is interested in what you have to say. You've also spent a few months "testing" whether or not your particular brand of knowledge is of interest to others before you've risked anything.

The people in your audience will appreciate that you took the time to share a tremendous amount of knowledge before you tried to sell them anything and you already know that they're part of your target market because you've given them multiple opportunities to opt in/out as you progress through each part of your business development.

You'll notice that the title of this section is "How to Start a Business With Just $0.10 in Your Pocket" but you haven't found out what to do with that $0.10 yet. Take the $0.10 and use it to print the required forms to create a Sole Proprietorship at your local library. You're now ready to become an official business – congratulations!

SEEK OUT COMMUNITY

Do you remember what it was like your first day of high school? College? Your first corporate job? You probably felt a mix of excitement and fear. You didn't know if people would like you, you were unsure of who your friends would be, but you knew you were ready to get started! Entrepreneurship is a similar feeling.

When you join an entrepreneur community (my favorites are the Savvy Business Owners' Community and the Rising Tide Society), you're "making yourself known" to thousands of other women and men who are also on the entrepreneurial journey. There are often local meet ups (like the Rising Tide Society Tuesdays Together meetings) where you can interact and build relationships with local entrepreneurs. The difference between high school, college, or a corporate job and entrepreneurship is that as entrepreneurs, we all have the same goal – grow our business. Not everybody has the same goal in those other settings. This common goal and common desired experience makes entrepreneurship and its associated communities a phenomenal place to meet people and maybe even come alive!

Are you curious how entrepreneurship could bring you to life? Consider this example:

A little over a year ago, two entrepreneurs were scrolling through the Savvy Business Owners' Facebook group. One was a graphic designer that had built up an incredible business doing work for Kansas City businesses and other entrepreneurs. The other was a photographer in Tulsa who had a knack for crafting beautiful imagery to preserve some of life's most precious moments. Both women felt like their business was missing something, but they weren't sure what it was. As they scrolled through the group, making connections, collaborating to help give someone advice on their new logo, and being a shoulder to lean on as someone else struggled with a difficult client situation, they became friends. That friendship blossomed into conversations about business, their dreams, and what they wanted most out of life. Soon thereafter, Think Creative Collective was born.

Today, Abagail and Emylee work together to maximize the incredible breadth of skills they share between them. Their social media accounts are flawless courtesy of Emylee's amazing photography skills and their downloadable PDFs are always drop dead gorgeous courtesy of Abagail's graphic design skills. Together, they run a business that is greater than the sum of their parts and impacts thousands of women on the entrepreneurial journey all because they made a connection in an entrepreneur community a little over a year ago.

Without the entrepreneurial community that exists online and all over the globe, relationships like the one that Abagail and Emylee have today wouldn't be possible. These two women are now running a business that brings them joy and they get to share that joy with their business partner on a daily basis! Remember when they each felt like something was missing from their business? It was one another.

What's the lesson here? There's something in your life today that you wish you had more of. There's space in your life for something that could very well bring out the best in you. For many people, it's joining a community of like minded peers and getting to experience the tremendous camaraderie that results from conversation. For you, it might be finding your next business partner when you didn't even know you were looking for one. Regardless of what it is, it's important to step out of your comfort zone, engage in community with others, and feel alive.

EMAIL MANAGEMENT

Ever wondered what you should be doing with incoming mail? Give these methods a try!

Filter incoming mail. When an email comes to my inbox, there are three different things that could happen to it. If it's a newsletter, it's automatically going to get rolled up in my daily Unroll.Me email. I have it set to come to my inbox at night, so at around 5pm every day, I get the previous day's email rollup. This is good because if there were any hot sales, it reduces my impulse purchases, and I'm tackling these newsletters after all the business tasks are done for the day. If it's a current client email, it gets flagged red, which tells me I need to take a look at it. If it's anything else, it lands in my inbox. Allie (my assistant) takes the first pass at my inbox so by the time I dive in, things have been trashed, filed, or moved to the "Dannie Please Review" inbox.

Manage mail once it's read. Believe it or not, I only have five main folders in my inbox. I used to get so annoyed scrolling down a long list of folders, so I have everything in five categories: LE Consulting Business (this is where my guest post, collaboration, proposal, etc. folders are), Current Clients, Past Clients (I archive clients here for two years and then delete the folder), Receipts (I sort receipts by year), and Secondary Businesses (Side Hustle Gal and my upcoming partnership with Rosemary Watson and TwigyPosts). Everything is in a subfolder inside one of those five folders. If a client has multiple projects with me, that client also has a separate subfolder for each project (i.e. Monique Melton hired me for her Book Launch PR and for general marketing - under the Monique Melton folder, there is a separate folder for each of these two projects).

Canned responses. I have quite a few different canned responses set up in Gmail to save me time and energy when responding (and to make life easier for Allie). I have canned responses pre-templated for sending a proposal (if needed), welcoming a client, outlining my policies and procedures, asking for reviews, and even for setting up partnership/collaboration opportunities.

SHARE YOUR KNOWLEDGE

Now that you've gained all of this tremendous knowledge about running a business, it's important to share that knowledge wildly. Why?

1: It establishes you as an expert and helps you display your knowledge. By sharing your knowledge wildly, whether it's in blog posts, on webinars, or even in free e-courses, people are able to gain an understanding for what you know and how you know it. This increases your level of expertise in their eyes and aids when trying to gain them as a client.

2: If you give that much away for free, they can expect even more as your client! You likely want to be seen as someone who has stellar service quality, under-promising and over-delivering for your clients. By giving away knowledge for free, you demonstrate your willingness to "pitch in and help" to potential clients.

3: It shows the quality of your work and acts like a portfolio for your business. In some industries, it can be hard to have a portfolio. For example, for us here at LE Consulting, it's hard to showcase a client's marketing success without doing an in depth case study. It might be hard for a business coach to show her clients' successes except through testimonials. Writing blog posts and sharing your knowledge can serve as a secondary portfolio and another tool for helping potential clients decide whether or not to hire you.

4. You'll have a body of work to share when applying for speaking engagements, guest blog spots, podcast interviews, and more! Everyone wants publicity, right? When pitching, applying for, or submitting to many of these opportunities, they'll either (a) request samples of past work (writing, speaking, etc.) or (b) check you out online. By having a blog and/or other sources where you give knowledge away freely, you're giving the reviewers something to look at when considering your submission. Win-win!

5. You'll feel good too! Do you ever go back to look at that paper you knocked out of the park freshman year of college? Or that art project that still makes you smile 10 years later? Imagine scrolling through blog posts you've written that are full of awesome content! It's a great feeling!

managing your team

Memoir by Amanda Cox Photography

Photography has played a vital role in my life. Growing up, my parents were always snapping photos – from holidays and special occasions, to the everyday moments in life, like picnics in the backyard in the summer and sledding in the winter. And so it was no surprise that I developed a fondness for photography. I can clearly recall packing a lunch and heading out into the woods surrounding my childhood home with my camera in tow, exploring and photographing the world around me for hours. Although I had this deep love for photography, it never occurred to me that I could turn it into a career one day. When the time came to go off to college, I did the sensible thing and went business school, with the goal of having a good job one day in order to make a nice living for myself.

After graduating from Concord University in West Virginia, with degrees in Management and Marketing, I went into Management with the Fortune 25 Company I worked for throughout my college years. During my time in Management, I discovered a deep love and passion for the people side of the business. Recruiting, interviewing, hiring, and training the newest associates were my favorite activities, and ones I did with great enthusiasm. Nearly two years into my career, the opportunity arose for me to specialize in the field of Human Resources, which I eagerly accepted.

Over the next eight years, I would hold positions as an exempt-level recruiter, head of the exempt-level training and development program for a 5,000+ person division of the company I worked for, and would eventually move on to work in HR Generalist roles for the last three years of my HR career. Throughout the years, I gained certifications to facilitate a dozen training courses, trained thousands of team members from the newest associates to Senior VPs, and was hand-selected by the company to work on 3 different small teams to develop major training programs that are still in use today. I also spent countless hours with Managers and Supervisors, counseling them on proper interviewing and hiring techniques, coaching them on how to handle conflict amongst team members, and working on investigations into various concerns. During my career, I continued my own education as well, achieving my Professional in Human Resources (PHR) and Society of Human Resource Management – Certified Professional (SHRM – CP) certifications. My HR career was thriving.

But it wasn't enough for me. Almost a decade after graduating college and starting my professional career, I decided to leave it all behind to start my own business. I walked away to forge my own path and bring my dreams to life, specifically, my dreams of being a professional photographer and owning my own business. Some thought I was crazy and that I was throwing away everything for which I had worked so hard; while others encouraged and supported me on this exciting new journey.

Since starting my own business, I don't feel like I've thrown anything away. In fact, the last 10 years of my life have truly helped prepare me to be a stronger, smarter, and more tenacious entrepreneur. From taking calculated risks, to making sound legal

148

decisions to protect my business and my family, to being prepared for things to come in the future; my background has equipped me to handle a great deal.

As you know, however, starting your own business is no easy feat. There are so many more things that I've learned along the way by experimenting and making mistakes as I go along. One trait that I've seen that's consistent amongst successful entrepreneurs and business owners is persistence. Sticking with something, even though you may feel as though nothing is going right, and everything is falling apart, is what sets a successful business owner apart from everyone else. And it's the same when growing, managing and leading a team. You're not going to know everything up front, but you need to have the persistence to learn, make smart decisions and grow.

Human Resources is such an integral part of any business – whether it's a Fortune 25 Company or a one (wo)man show. Although you may have the best intentions and are a kind-hearted leader with loads of integrity, knowing your legal responsibilities and obligations as an employer will be essential. Managing and leading a team is not simply limited to a job description and some initial training. It incorporates a host of other requirements on the employers end, such as knowing wage and hours laws, overtime regulations, employment taxes, disability/workers' compensation regulations, health care benefits requirements, and so much more, which will all become part of your wheelhouse as you add team members. This will all depend on the size and structure of your team, as well as where your business is located, too.

Bringing team members into your business is a huge responsibility that should not be taken lightly. Doing your research upfront by talking with your accountant, attorney, and even an HR pro, will help you prepare for the financial and legal requirements you will take on, as well as the actual hiring, onboarding and training processes you'll be undertaking. As a small business owner, hiring team members is an area where I would recommend you do your due diligence in researching and learning about federal, state and local employment laws to ensure you understand your obligations, requirements and level of commitment before you place an advertisement for a team member. It will save you so much time, stress, frustration, and potentially, money and lawsuits.

Managing and leading a team of people can be such a rewarding experience. Doing it legally and responsibly will make that experience so much more enjoyable for both parties, providing you with the time and energy you need to focus on your growing team and business. One thing is for certain, though; it's sure to be an amazing new adventure in growing your business!

- *Ashley Cox*

Ashley Cox is the owner of sproutHR, where she helps creative entrepreneurs learn all about how to hire, train, and grow a thriving team. Whether you feel like you're in way over your head hiring your first team member, or you're looking for someone to help you create a strategic long-term plan, she partners with you as your personal HR expert! You can find her at www.sprouthr.co

PART ONE: HIRING

Deciding who to hire. Deciding who to hire is a two part process. First, you need to determine whether or not you're ready to hire someone. Second, you need to determine what kind of "someone" you need to hire. Are you ready? Do you have at least five hours of work each week you want to outsource? Is all of that work within a single category (you could hire one person to handle it)? For example, if you have two hours of Excel work and three hours of marketing work, you'll want to hire one person (such as a VA) to handle both or wait until you have five or more hours in one category to hire an Excel or marketing specialist.

Who to hire? If you're looking to hire someone for the first time, an excellent choice would be a VA. They're typically multi-skilled and can handle a variety of different tasks until you're ready to specialize in terms of who is a part of your team. Having at least five hours of work a week is important - the average VA runs $15-$25/hour and you'll want to give them enough work to make it worth their time to work with you as well. In this case, $300-$500/month is a good starting point and will make the working relationship good for both parties.

Disclaimer: There are always exceptions to every "rule". You may be ready to hire some help even if you have less than 5 hours of work per week to give them. You just may have to either (a) pay the VA or other hire a higher hourly wage or (b) buy a bank of hours to start. These are different solutions that some VAs or other assistants use to manage lower hourly commitments.

Deciding when to hire. Deciding when to hire comes down to your business and your needs. You may be ready before you even go live with your business or you might not need to hire help until your company has been around for 4+ years. One element is whether or not you have enough work to offer an employee / contractor / service provider (see above) and another is your own availability. If you have the time to dedicate all the hours you need to in and on your business, go for it! If you don't have the time, hiring help will allow you to get your business off the ground or to the next level much more quickly.

Are you ready to take on the additional burdens of hiring help? When you hire help, you may need additional office space, equipment, and/or software licenses. For example, if you're a graphic designer and you're hiring a VA, you may have to provide them access to Adobe Illustrator, which will run you $19.99/month (for a CC account). Will the benefits from hiring help outweigh the added costs? Truthfully, nobody from the outside can tell you when it's time to hire help. There are many factors to consider and only you can decide what's right for your business.

Interviewing. The first and most critical point about interviewing help (whether it's actually interviewing a potential employee or vetting a contractor / service provider) is to not sell your company first. This might sound strange - but consider this: by spending too much time upfront talking about your company and not enough time asking good questions, your candidates can use the information to hone their personal sales pitches and reduce the amount of "transparency" you get from them.

The next critical point about interviewing help is to ask the right interview questions. Open-ended questions always trump closed-ended questions in the interview process because they provide more insight into the candidate or service provider. For example:

Question: ''Tell me about a time when you had to lead your team in a new direction.'' Candidates will have to provide you with one or more challenges that they faced and the specific steps they took with their team to meet them. It will be clear to you if they fudge their answer and if the experience is genuine.

Closed-ended interview questions really don't do much for you. For example:

Question: ''Do you consider yourself to be a leader?'' This question lets candidates off the hook by allowing them to give a one-word (or at least very limited) answer. You have learned nothing.

Open ended questions encourage conversation and will provide a better interview or screening experience. on interviewing and hiring.

Onboarding. Your business will need the processes, procedures, and organization in place to handle an influx of employees or help. All new hires (whether they're actual employees or just contractors/service providers) will need orientation, training, and management. There might be additional federal or state legal requirements should the employed staff size expand to certain numbers.

Want to explain your processes quickly? Create "record screen" videos that capture exactly how you do things, like setting up your MailChimp campaigns or organizing your files.

Want to provide passwords in an organized manner? Try a tool like LastPass to organize passwords, generate random passwords, and more.

Want to give your VA email access? Don't let them login to your email. Either set them up with their own email (assistant@yourcompany.com, va@yourcompany.com, etc) or set up their email as an alias and have all emails sent to that address forwarded to their personal email. Don't let them log in to your email until trust is established and they've been working for you for a proven amount of time.

PART TWO: DELEGATING

Congratulations! You've decided what role you want to hire for and when you're ready to get started. You've figured out how to interview and hire someone and how to make sure they're onboarded properly. Now it's time to determine what tasks you'll assign them and how!

What is "effective delegation?" London Business School professor John Hunt notes that only 30 percent of managers think they can delegate well, and of those, only one in three is considered a good delegator by his or her subordinates. This means only about one manager in ten really knows how to empower others. This is scary!

The absolute best tool I could recommend for delegation is Jan Yager's book Work Less, Do More. Here are some of her tips and strategies for delegating: Choose what tasks you are willing to delegate. You should be using your time on the most critical tasks for the business, and the tasks that only you can do. Delegate what you can't do, and what doesn't interest you. For example, non-computer types should consider delegating their social media, website, and SEO activities.

Trust those to whom you delegate. It always starts with trust. Along with trust, you also have to give the people to whom you delegate the chance to do a job their way. Of course the work must be done well, but your way or the highway is not the right way. Give clear assignments and instructions. The key is striking the right balance between explaining so much detail that the listener is insulted, and not explaining enough for someone to understand.

Avoid reverse delegation. Some team members try to give a task back to the manager, if they don't feel comfortable, or are attempting to dodge responsibility. Don't accept it except in extreme cases. In the long run, every team member needs to learn or leave.

Delegating is scary, especially for entrepreneurs. You've built your business from the ground up and you've put in the blood, sweat, and tears to make it the success it is today. Letting go of a few tasks is the hurdle keeping you from that next rung of success - you can only achieve so much if your plate is full.

Determining what to delegate. I want you to grab a blank piece of paper (or use the space below) and mark off four quadrants. Label one "Important and Essential," one "Important and Non-Essential," one "Unimportant and Essential," and one "Unimportant and Non-Essential."

Now, take some time to dump all the business tasks you do on a daily basis into this set of quadrants. Not sure what you do in your business on a daily basis? Use this Time Excavation Spreadsheet to write down every task you do in a week (reference emails and files if you need to).

Once you've completed the brain dump, the very first step is to look at everything in the Unimportant and Non-Essential quadrant. Why are you doing these tasks? What are they? Are they necessary for the success of your business? If not, eliminate them from your task list. If they are, move them to another quadrant, as they don't belong in this one.

Next, look at the Important and Non-Essential and Unimportant and Essential quadrants. These are going to be your sweet spot for delegation. Grab a highlighter (or two highlighters if you're hiring more than one person) and highlight the tasks you want to hand off. Next, assign an estimated amount of time you spend on these items each week. Total them up and you now have your task list for your new hire(s) and the expected amount of time you'll need them per week.

Explaining and assigning. Now that you know what you're delegating and to whom, it's time to introduce your new hires to their assignments! Create a "job description" or other document that outlines the weekly tasks you're assigning each new hire, along with the expected time commitment per task. Next, gather a list of resources they'll need to complete these tasks (i.e. if you need your VA to create graphics in Canva, she'll also need your Canva login details - place these on her sheet next to the Canva task).

157

This document becomes your covenant of sorts between you and your new hire - you've laid out the expectations and the tasks for their role very clearly, it's their opportunity to ask questions and get started!

PART THREE: MANAGING

Congratulations! You've finished your Time Excavation, you've completed your four quadrants, and you're ready to let your team spread their wings and step back and start managing. In reality, you're still swamped with tasks, but the fact that you have a team in place should feel good and should make you feel (at least a little) lighter.

The difference between a boss and a leader. If you go to school for Human Resources, Organizational Leadership, or even just a general Business degree, one of the first conversations you'll have in your management class is "what is the difference between a boss and a leader?" Various branches of the military teach this as one of their very first critical lessons in Officer Candidate School. It's applicable for creative entrepreneurs too, believe it or not! You want to make sure that these wonderful people you're working with are being developed and being given opportunities to develop their skills further. Working with you is great, but they likely want more than just a paycheck about the experience. You have an opportunity to help them develop new and awesome skills!

Managing fellow creatives. Managing creatives requires a different approach than say, managing a financial analyst. I've broken my recommendations for managing your team into five segments below:

Manage attentively. Make sure to schedule weekly (or depending on hours worked - biweekly) check-ins with the members of your team. This is important for providing feedback, assigning projects that aren't routine, and taking some time to listen to what they might be struggling with. This also gives them an opportunity to share their unique successes with you.

Manage strategically. Your team has a variety of skills. The person you've hired as your VA might also have awesome copywriting skills that you can use. Make sure you're asking your team about other skills they have that they'd like to utilize. Give them the opportunity to "flex their muscles" and try projects that aren't in their normal wheelhouse. They'll love you for it.

Manage thoughtfully. Just like you appreciate when your clients give open ended feedback (instead of directives like "move this exactly .05mm to the left"), your employees appreciate the same. Unless it's a project that requires direct approaches to feedback ("you added 3 and 4 and got 9 - the answer is 7"), give them the opportunity to come up with their own solutions to achieve the goals you've laid out. You'll get better results from them and they'll be happier and more motivated employees.

Manage intentionally. When there is an issue (and there will be one, no employee is 100% perfect and that's okay), handle it directly and quickly. You don't want to let your disappointment fester and your employees will appreciate the timely feedback. You'll have a better working relationship too, because the honesty and transparency will be evident in your relationship.

Manage planfully. Having weekly (or monthly) team meetings to talk about previous results and lay out the plan for the upcoming months is a great plan! It'll help you be strategic in your thinking (because you'll have to prep for the meetings) but it'll also help your employees feel included.

PART FOUR: STREAMLINING

You've figured out the difference between a boss and a leader and you're ready to lead your employees. You understand that managing a creative is different than managing someone in a more analytical role. You've checked into some awesome management tools and you're ready to start streamlining.

Why streamline when you're hiring a team? It's really exciting that you're at a place to hire a team, but the last thing I want you to do is waste money. Now that you've hired your team and started managing them, it's time to re-evaluate your processes and what you have your team working on to make sure that your money is being spent wisely.

This process is done in the "corporate world" through annual performance reviews (but rest assured that's not what I'm suggesting for you). During this annual performance review time, a manager looks at her employees' work over the past 12 months, considers what went well and what didn't, and looks at goals to see how many were accomplished and which ones are still unfinished.

This same process can be applied to your business as a creative, just in a different manner. Open up your calendar and mark down two times (January and July) or four times (March, June, September, and December) to do a review of your business. This is not a review of your employees (but it can be if that's something you're interested in doing) but a review of your business and processes.

What to review: are the processes below (a) too long, (b) ineffective, or (c) redundant?

- Client acquisition and onboarding (how long from first contact to signed contract / paid deposit?)
- Client intake (how long does it take a client to get you all the information you need to get started? Is there anything you can do to speed up this process?)
- Business Management (this is the amount of time you spend working on your business, not in it. Are you spending enough time to get everything done - bookkeeping, trademark upkeep, blogging, etc.)
- Design Process (how long does it take end-to-end to complete a project with a client, regardless of what your services are).

- Any other process that you frequently replicate in your business.

When you have team members, it's even more critical that your processes are consistent each time and that they follow a logical sequence. An added benefit of evaluating and upgrading your processes is the additional value you'll be offering your clients because they're getting your very best work every single time they talk to you!

what happens now

If you've made it here, thank you. You've read my labor of love cover to cover and I appreciate it tremendously. I'm sure you're wondering "what happens now?"

The answer is that **it's time for you to fly.** You picked up this book because you're an entrepreneur, you're a strong woman, you're interested in business, or a variety of other reasons. It's time to act on that motivation! Write a plan. Come up with a strategy to get started. Organize your thoughts and just take that first step!

If you are looking for support in your journey, consider joining the Side Hustle Gal community on Facebook. We'd love to have you!

facebook.sidehustlegal.com

acknowledgements

This book would not have been possible without the amazing support of some truly incredible people! This book may be published under my name but it is truly collaboration with some of the greatest entrepreneurial minds I've had the pleasure of connecting with.

First, to my amazing **collaborators and contributors**, you rock! This book would not be real, published, or in readers' hands without your honesty and vulnerability. You allow this book to offer so much more than one person's perspective and I'm so pleased to have had you on this journey with me! In order of appearance:

Melissa & Adam Schmidt of eMBee Events
www.embee-events.com

Cinnamon Wolfe of Cinnamon Wolfe Photography
www.cinnamonwolfephotography.com

Abagail Pumphrey & Emylee Williams of Think Creative Collective www.thinkcreativecollective.com

Britny West of The Traveling Mindset Coach
www.britnywest.com

Kat Karpoff of Soapbox Creative Consulting
www.soapboxcreativeconsulting.com

Reid & Brittany Photography
www.reidandbrittany.com

Emily Walker of Chloe + Isabel
www.chloeandisabel.com/boutique/emilywalker

Kyrsten & Kelly Sherwood of Copper Kettle Co
www.ckc.io

Maggie Giele of Maggie Giele Digital Strategy
www.maggiegiele.com

Ashley Mackey Cox of Ashley Cox Photography
www.ashcoxphoto.com

A special thank you to the girls at **Think Creative Collective**. You've been some of my biggest fans since I splashed out of the corporate entrepreneur space and onto the creative entrepreneur scene a year ago. You helped me transition from small town agency to big time creative entrepreneur. Your willingness to share resources without fear has been one of the greatest blessings of my entrepreneurial journey. I am forever grateful for you and your amazing grace.

A massive thank you to **those who have challenged** me and what I'm doing or who have sought to duplicate my efforts. This book wouldn't have been finished without the motivation you offered me to push through my blocks and get my message out there. A wise woman once said, *"when we as creatives stand in our truth, our words have power. Our voice is defined. Our real-hand-to-god-follow-you-to-the-grave tribe comes out of the woodwork to support us."* You taught me that not only is there a market for my story, but there are people that want to hear it too. I'm so grateful to have found my true tribe. At the end of the day, we are all after the same goal and that is a goal of community over competition. This book aims to stay true to this goal without fail.

To the book designer of my dreams (and a book collaborator and my dear friend) **Kyrsten Sherwood of Copper Kettle Co**. You blew my mind with every concept for the book cover and I know it would not look nearly as amazing without your work. You're an incredible human and I truly appreciate your contributions to the book more than words could ever express.

To my wonderful book editor, **Stuart Chapman** (with help from Janet Chapman). Thank you for reading the manuscript with a magnifying glass, for your loving notes marked in red pen, and for putting up with the million times I changed my mind on dates and plans. This book sounds the way it should – eloquent and polished – because of your hard work and efforts.

To my mom, **Cyndi.** You are the reason I have become the successful woman I am today. You are the reason I have a place to call home, a family that loves me, and roots to keep me grounded. I owe you my life.

To **my family**, who supported me through this "crazy idea" of writing a book on top of everything else I do in life, thank you. Thank you for being my unofficial editors, my life coaches, my support system, and the people I can always count on.

To **my friends** – Kasia, Emily, Anthony, Cameron, Taylor, and everyone else (you know who you are), for tolerating countless messages and questions and pestering, asking for ideas and advice and reminders of memories we've experienced. For supporting me through the late nights full of tears and anger and frustration. For sending me flowers just to cheer me up. For reminding me day in and day out that there's more to life than writing and working. You are all amazing!

To **those who entered and exited my life over the course of this book** – The Side Hustle Gal came together so quickly. I started writing in late 2015 and here we are, less than a year later, and this book is finished. I am so grateful for those of you who passed through my life during this time, whether we met and parted ways over the course of the past year or you simply moved on to bigger and better things, I am grateful for the influence you had on my life.

To my tremendous business coaches, **Courtney Romano and Kat Karpoff.** You lovely ladies rock and I thank you so much for all you've done to push me and support me as I worked on this endeavor. You've been real and reminded me that my excuses don't exist. You've said day after day that I have to *"face [my] fears and start writing. Get [my] shit down on the page. Be precious with who [I] let see it. Pour [my] whole self into it."* What you see here is my whole self. I have nothing left to give. Your support and your willingness to push me into the light has been one of the greatest pieces of support I've received throughout my entrepreneurial journey. *Thank you.*

To my "Thailand Crew" – **Britny West, Kate Curtis, and Christiana Whitley.** You are some of the greatest humans on this planet. You managed to push me towards the finish line all while not laughing at me for my lack of clothes or cleanliness during those few days in Thailand I was without luggage. I am so grateful for your continued motivation, support, love, and most of all – YOGA. I would not have survived the creation of this book without yoga.

To **Stephanie de Geus**, the copywriting wizard. Thank you for helping tremendously with the framework of the book, for helping manage my blog strategy so I could focus more on this project, and for generally being a support system during the book's infancy. You are fantastic!

To my **LE Consulting team**, for tolerating all the overlap between LEPC and the Side Hustle Gal. For taking on a bigger burden because I am spread so thin. For being my OG book customers and dear friends.

To **my clients** for knowing and honoring the fact that I was writing a book while working with you and loving me anyway. You are amazing, each and every one of you!

Finally, to all the **Side Hustle Gals** out there. This book is 100%, no questions asked, hands down for you. I wrote this book because I was frustrated. I was angry at how little support there was for part time entrepreneurs. I was concerned that the only path for a part time entrepreneur was to "ditch the 9-5" and that there was no other option that was considered acceptable. We are working together, you and I, to change that mindset, no matter how long it takes or how hard this journey might be.

I'm here to tell you that every. single. female. entrepreneur. is worthy. We are all strong. We are all brave. Entrepreneurship (regardless the shape, form, size, or color) is hard. Entrepreneurship is not for the weak. I'm here to tell you that I own two successful businesses and I still have a full time job. The truth is that women who are part time entrepreneurs (and I really do believe that word is a misnomer) are **ROCKSTARS**. We are **strong**. We are **capable**. It's time we stand together and recognize that we are a **force to be reckoned with.**

this is for you.

questions for discussion

To get a list of discussion questions and resources for leading a group through The Side Hustle Gal, visit discussion.sidehustlegal.com.

Dannie Fountain is a marketing consultant and the Founder of LE Consulting. She has worked in marketing for brands such as Whirlpool, H&R Block, and Mr. Kate. Her greatest passion is traveling the world - she's been to 21 countries (4 continents) and half the US so far, always with a trip on the horizon. She's a certified scuba diver and has her student pilot certification and those skills are evident in her well-rounded approach to marketing.

Dannie works with entrepreneurs to brainstorm, strategize, and implement marketing plans and processes to better their business. Her work also includes creating strategies for hiring and managing a team as a creative entrepreneur. She's also the author of a series of successful e-courses. Dannie is a regular guest contributor and speaker on marketing and the creative entrepreneur's struggle with hiring worldwide.

www.sidehustlegal.com
www.leconsulting.org // www.styledmarketingcourse.com